Slurping Through Europe

Slurping
Through Europe

200 Tasty Soup Recipes from around Europe

REGIS ROBINSON

ashfield
PRESS

First published in 2005 by

ASHFIELD PRESS • DUBLIN • IRELAND

ISBN: 1 901658 60 0

ACKNOWLEDGEMENTS
The author thanks the following for their help and assistance in compiling this book:
George Morrison, Miriam ffrench Mullen, David Browne, Barbara Browne,
Simon Robinson, Jonathan Williams, John Davey, Judith Elmes, Susan Waine,
Catherine Sheridan, Peter Caviston and Caviston's Emporium, Meadows and Byrne,
Lynne Oliver, The Food Time Line, Angela Burdick.

This book is typeset by Ashfield Press in 12.5 on 16 point Dante
Designed by SUSAN WAINE
Illustrated by ALWYN GILLESPIE
Photography by ASHFIELD PRESS
Printed in Ireland by ßETAPRINT LIMITED, DUBLIN

Contents

7

Introduction

I suppose soup is the immediate by-product of mankind's earliest attempts to tenderise meat and vegetables by boiling them. The method used, I am sure, was to find a deep hollow in a rocky area, fill it with water, heat some stones in a fire and roll them into the water with a branch. The next step was to chop up the raw meat, bones and vegetables with flint cutters and toss them into this natural pot. Once the water came to the boil, more super-heated stones were added to keep the brew at boiling point. When they figured that the meat and vegetables were tender enough to eat, they were left with a stone stockpot brimming with delicious soup, which they probably scooped out with large seashells or gourds.

Haute cuisine it was not, but the millennia sped by and the Stone Age became the Bronze Age, cavemen became hut-dwellers, tribes became kingdoms and kingdoms became empires. It was then that sophisticated craftsmen began to produce pots and pans from metal, and bowls, cups and plates from clay. It was also the time that our ancestors learned to till the land and breed animals for the table.

And there was always soup...soup, no matter what!

We know about Greek cuisine when Greece ruled the known world through the writings of Apicus, a Roman gourmet, in his book written in the last century B.C. Several fires at the Library of Alexandria destroyed almost all written records of life in ancient Greece over the long period of its existence, culminating in its final destruction by fire in the seventh century A.D.

All things Greek were highly admired by the Romans, including their cuisine, which had a considerable influence on Roman cooking. Apicus also gives us the earliest recorded soup recipe from a chef who called it Pultes Julianae or Julian Potage, no doubt in honour of Julius Caesar. There is an updated version of this recipe on page 115.

By the time the Emperor Hadrian came along, the Romans were

more interested in maintaining their borders than in expanding them, as they had been doing for a thousand years. They were afraid that the so-called Barbarians, who for the most part were nomadic peoples from the vastness of what we now call Russia, would destroy their civilized way of life. All these nomads had their own developed cultures and many of them became Roman citizens centuries before the Rhine was breached in the fourth century and the Barbarians overran the whole of Italy. It is not difficult to understand the influence this had on farming practices and food in general for the next thousand years.

We Europeans had no peppers (Capsicums), no Indian corn, no beans and no tomatoes. Nor did we have the eponymous potato to use in our soups before Columbus discovered the New World. Yet within a few hundred years, all these things were grown throughout the Old World to augment the onions, cabbage, turnips, carrots, peas, wheat and beet that have since been used in traditional soups.

Mind you, the same thing happened the other way around in what has come to be known as the Columbian Exchange. The New World got our ingredients and we got theirs.

In this book, I have made all the recipes historically accurate but have applied today's preparation and cooking techniques, and have used canned and frozen foods in some cases. I find that when it comes to soup preparation, canned tomatoes and beans, for example, lose little or nothing in quality and flavour compared to the fresh article. I know the purists will throw up their hands in shock-horror but cooking can be fun, so why make it difficult? You'll find most of the recipes in this book aim at simplifying the art of making a good soup.

In all the recipes I have used the ingredients that have always been the traditional garnishes, but I have also given a glossary of many other, sometimes more interesting, garnishes that are worth trying. Basic soups are basic soups, but your creative imagination can add another dimension to many of them.

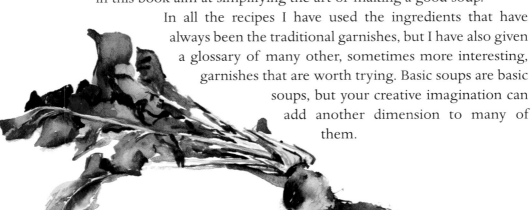

Useful hints and help

A fter 40 years or so as a chef, I have learnt a few things about basic cooking which are worth thinking about. For example, you will find the best way to get dissolved fat off the surface of your soup is to carefully ladle the hot soup and fat from the pot into a fat separator – a glass jug with a spout at the bottom which allows the soup to flow out while the fat remains in the jug. Thus you end up with fat-free soup which you pour back into the saucepan. You can also allow the soup to go cold, chill it overnight and then remove the solidified fat with a slotted spoon. If you have been using butter in your recipe, serve croutons or oven-dried crusts with the soup because they will absorb the butter. Butter is too expensive to throw away.

Whereas I heartily recommend the use of real stocks in my recipes, there can be no doubt that there is a place in your larder for high quality stock cubes of chicken and beef, fish sauces and meat extracts such as Bovril. Tubes of tomato paste, garlic purée, dried porcini mushroom pieces, celery salt, too. I go for French stock cubes, Asian fish sauces and British meat extracts. A bottle of dry sherry, dry white wine and some cooking brandy won't go amiss. I find red wine in soup tricky. It gives a heavy, luscious quality, which your soup can do without, whereas a well-judged dash of dry sherry gives many soups a lovely lift. Good quality dried herbs and spices are available, too, in most supermarkets.

The quickest soup ever can be made with a crumbled beef or chicken stock cube, a dessertspoon of tomato paste and a quarter teaspoon of garlic purée, all stirred into 500ml of boiling water. You get two bowls of very tasty soup from this piece of legerdemain in almost no time. You can even thicken it with two teaspoons of cornflour dissolved in a little cold water and stirred in at boiling point. Shake in some celery salt, too, for further excitement.

Butchers usually give away bones without charge to their customers, as do fish shops. Farmed salmon, although it cannot compete in flavour and texture with wild salmon, is an excellent fish in its own right and can be satisfactory in some soups.

Buy yourself a good stockpot, make your basic stocks and freeze them in measured plastic containers. You are halfway to a great soup. My parsimonious mother kept a stockpot going all the time when I was a youngster. There were no deep freezes in those days, so nothing edible in the house was ever thrown out and free bones from the butcher were a great delight to her. Almost everything went into this pot and the extraordinary thing about it was that the soup always tasted exactly the same: delicious beyond description. Mind you, she did not go as far as mixing fish with meat – unthinkable in the first half of the last century, when she was young. Game carcasses mixed with beef, lamb and chicken bones, bread, potato peelings, left-over vegetables of all kinds and the devil knows what else produced this wonderful soup in the winter.

There seems to be a very remarkable piece of chemistry that goes on in soup when it is left overnight. It always tastes better the following day. I remember the first restaurant I was involved in with two friends who, having told me they wanted to open a nightspot which served good food, asked would I be interested. I had been a pretty good amateur cook and my answer was 'hallelujah', seeing that I had just had my chequebook flambéed in an unwise expedition into the film business.

I had two soups there among the starters, Onion Soup and

Shellfish Bisque, which got better and better in the bain-marie as they were topped up from hour to hour. Indeed these soups were so popular that they remained on the menu for the ten years that I was chef there and I am glad to be able say that it was that successful introduction into the restaurant business that prompted me to open my own restaurant later, and, later still, to become a caterer, sometime food writer and lecturer.

I keep the best bits of advice to the last. All chefs will tell you that the production of good food for the table is all in the preparation. This is why you will find that in the list of ingredients in all my recipes I have specified how each ingredient should be prepared before you get down to the actual cooking.

By the way, these days you can use your microwave oven to sweat vegetables. Chop them and cook them with a little butter and water in a covered bowl at full power for five minutes.

And always remember, quality ingredients beget quality soups.

Ideal Kitchen Equipment

plastic bowls	fridge
freezer	colander
liquidiser or food processor	sieve
wooden spoon	ladle
slotted spoon	wire skimmer
Paris whisk	stockpot
large saucepan	medium saucepan
frying pan	fat separator
measuring jug	measuring spoon
pepper mill*	gas baffler, if you are using natural gas**

*   *Always use freshly milled black pepper.*

**   *Unlike coal gas, natural gas can extinguish at a very low (simmer) flame in older hobs.*

Stock

uildings without a firm foundation have been known to collapse into a meaningless mess. You'll find that it can be much the same with soup. All great soups must have a firm foundation and this is something you can create in your own stockpot in your own kitchen.

Admittedly, there are many stock cubes and stock jars on sale in every supermarket and grocery shop in the world. Many of them can have a use in cooking, but nothing will ever take the place of the real thing – a homemade, basic stock.

There is nothing complicated about this process, and the important ingredients are readily available, either free or at an inexpensive price.

You make *white stock* from raw poultry, beef, veal or game.

To make *brown stock*, you roast the bones, which will give you colour as well as extra flavour.

For *fish stock*, your local fish shop will supply you with the bones and heads left over from the filleting process.

Bouillon comes from the stock left when you cook meat or poultry in water. It is an important component in many soups.

Court bouillon is the stock you get when you poach vegetables in water. It is used as a component of other stocks.

Vegetable stock is made by poaching vegetables in court bouillon or as described below.

Glacé is a jelly or syrup concentrate, which you get by reducing meat or fish stocks.

Beef Stock

Ingredients

1.5kg	meaty beef bones, cracked
1.5kg	shin beef, cubed
2	medium onions, skin on, chopped
2	large carrots, peeled and chopped
2	celery stalks, trimmed and chopped
1	leek, green parts on, trimmed and chopped
4	whole garlic cloves, unpeeled
1	bunch of parsley stems, chopped
2	medium tomatoes, de-seeded and chopped
$^1/_2$	tsp dried thyme
2	bay leaves
2	cloves
1 tsp	rock salt
8	black peppercorns

Method

Preheat your oven to 130°C. Brush the cracked bones and cubed shin beef with heated vegetable oil, put them in a roasting tin and roast for 10 minutes. Heat one tablespoon of vegetable oil in a medium saucepan, drop in all the vegetables and stir them about with a wooden spoon until they are coated with the oil. Pour all this into the roasting tin and roast for 30 minutes. Lift the bones, beef and vegetables from the roasting tin and put them into a clean stockpot. Pour off the fat from the roasting tin and place it on two medium-hot burners on the hob. Pour on 500ml water and allow it to boil for a few minutes, scraping all the browned residue into the water. Let it cool, then pour it into the stockpot, along with enough cold water to cover the ingredients by 5cms, and bring it slowly to the boil. Skim off the scum or foam that rises to the top, since it contains impurities that will cloud the stock. Drop in the parsley stems, thyme, bay leaf, peppercorns and cloves, and simmer gently, uncovered, for 4 to 6 hours, topping it up with water from time to time to maintain the original level. Allow to cool, and pour the stock through a colander into a large bowl. Dispose of all the solids, put the bowl into your fridge and when any remaining fat solidifies on top, remove it. Pour the chilled stock into measured plastic containers, cover and freeze for future use.

Chicken Stock

Ingredients

1kg	chicken carcass, wings, neck and bones
2	carrots, chopped
2	onions, sliced
2	celery stalks, chopped
12	black peppercorns
5	cloves
10	parsley sprigs
1	large bay leaf

Method

Put all the ingredients into your stockpot, pour on 2 litres of cold water and bring it to the boil. Skim off all the scum or foam from the top and simmer uncovered for 60 minutes. Pour the stock through a colander into a large bowl and dispose of the solids. Allow to cool and put the bowl into your fridge. When the fat solidifies on top, remove it. Pour the chilled stock into measured plastic containers and freeze for future use.

Veal Stock

Ingredients

2kg	veal knuckles
1	medium onion, sliced
3	celery stalks, diced
1	medium carrot, diced
1	bay leaf
6	parsley stems
8	white peppercorns
6	whole cloves

Method

Put all the ingredients into your stockpot, pour on 2 litres of water and bring to the boil. Skim off any scum or foam and simmer uncovered for about 3 hours or until the volume is reduced by half. Allow to cool and skim again. Strain the stock into a bowl and dispose of the solids. Freeze in measured plastic containers for future use.

Fish Stock

Ingredients

1kg	fish trimmings, bones and heads, gills removed
1	onion, chopped
1	carrot, chopped
1	celery stalk, leaves on, chopped
1	twist of lemon peel
1	bay leaf
250ml	dry white wine

Salt and white pepper

Method

Put all the ingredients into your stockpot, pour on 1 litre of cold water and the wine and bring to the boil. Simmer uncovered for exactly 20 minutes – any longer will cause the stock to cloud. Skim, strain into a bowl through cloth and freeze in measured plastic containers.

Basic Vegetable Stock

Ingredients

5	carrots, chopped
2	celery stalks, leaves on, chopped
1	garlic head, cut in two
	peel of 2 medium potatoes
1	small turnip, sliced
1	bunch of parsley
1	bay leaf
6	black peppercorns
1 tsp	Salt

Method

Put all the ingredients into your stockpot, pour on 2 litres of cold water and bring to the boil. Skim and simmer gently, uncovered, for 60 minutes. Strain, dispose of the solids, skim again and freeze in measured plastic containers. This yields 1.5 litres. Double the ingredients for 3 litres.

Clarifying

For each litre of stock, you will need 1 lightly beaten egg white and the eggshell that has been crushed with a rolling pin. Pour the stock at room temperature into your saucepan and stir in the egg whites and crushed eggshell. Put the saucepan on to a low flame and allow it to come slowly to a very gentle simmer, without stirring or agitating it in any way. At this stage the impurities will be absorbed into the egg mix and will rise to the surface of the stock. Do not be tempted to skim off this scum. You may, however, push it gently aside to check that the stock is just simmering. If it boils, it will ruin the clarifying process. Simmer for 10 to 15 minutes, then carefully remove the saucepan from the hob and let it stand for an hour. Soak a piece of cloth in hot water, wring it out and use it to line your sieve. Pushing the scum aside, ladle the clarified liquid into the lined sieve. Let it cool, uncovered, and refrigerate it in tightly closed containers until you are ready to use it. It will keep for 4 days. Alternatively, freeze in measured plastic containers.

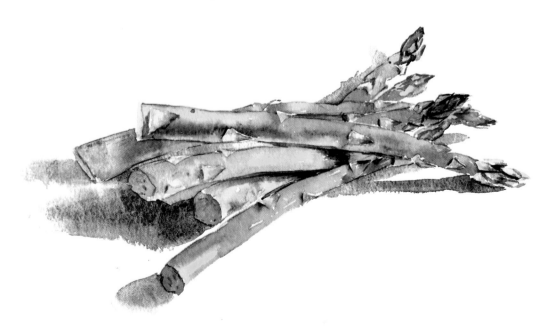

Garnishes

Although you will find that each of my recipes in this book have established garnishes, this list of other suggestions should tickle your imagination and give you some fun.

Meat and Poultry

pepperoni, cut in rounds

chorizo, cut in rounds

small meat or chicken quenelles (see p.193)

cooked cocktail sausages

finely cut ribbons of leaf vegetables

sweated matchsticks of root vegetables

cooked long-grained rice

cooked vermicelli

cooked egg noodles

cooked small pastas, such as route, anellini, stellini farfalle or
    tagliatelle

cooked puréed meat, bound in béchamel sauce

diced vegetables, sautéed in butter

cooked asparagus tips

glazed onions (see p. 195)

hard-boiled eggs, chopped

small cooked ravioli or tortellini with various stuffings

freshly grated Parmesan cheese

thin ribbons of cooked ham

puréed cooked beans

pea purée

sauerkraut, squeezed dry, rinsed and drained

Avgolemono sauce (see p. 192)

cooked sweetbreads, sliced

suet dumplings (see p. 63)

egg-bound dumplings (see p. 43)

matzo balls (see pp. 118-19)

Fish

Rouille sauce (see p.194)
cooked shrimps, shelled
cold water prawns, shelled
cooked Pacific prawns, thinly sliced
red or black lumpfish roe in sour cream
white fish quenelles
poached oysters, cockles, mussels or clams
cooked egg noodles
cooked small pasta
cooked vermicelli
Avgolemono sauce (see p. 192)

Vegetable

ribbons of leaf vegetables, sweated in butter
long-grained rice
vermicelli
cooked egg noodles
cooked tagliatelle
sautéed diced vegetables
stoned olives
pea or bean purée
Avgolemono sauce (see p. 192)
cooked asparagus tips
dried curd (see p. 193)
matzo balls (see pp. 118-19)
egg-bound dumplings (see p. 43)

Oven Temperature Conversion Chart

Gas Mark	1	275°F	140°C
	2	300°F	150°C
	3	325°F	170°C
	4	350°F	180°C
	5	375°F	190°C
	6	400°F	200°C
	7	425°F	220°C
	8	450°F	230°C
	9	475°F	240°C

Bean Jahni Soup *Jani Me Fasule Supë*

ALBANIA

●*Tirana*

Ingredients *(Serves 4)*

420g	can of white beans with the juice	1 tbsp	lemon juice
750ml	chicken stock	1 tbsp	chopped parsley
125g	diced onion	1 tbsp	chopped mint
125ml	olive oil	1	Jalapeno chilli, de-seeded and finely chopped
2 tbsp	tomato juice	Salt	

Method

Sauté the diced onions in the olive oil until they begin to colour. Add the beans with the juice, the parsley, chilli and lemon juice. Cook over a medium flame until it thickens somewhat (about 10 minutes), stirring continuously. Pour on the chicken stock, drop in half of the mint and bring to the boil. Skim, cover and simmer for 20 minutes more. Serve in bowls garnished with the remaining chopped mint.

Veal Soup *Mish Viçi Supë*

Ingredients *(Serves 4)*

		1	bunch of parsley stalks, finely chopped
500g	veal fillet, in the piece		
12	small new potatoes	2	stalks of celery, finely sliced
16	pickling onions, peeled		
1	litre veal stock	Chopped parsley	
		Salt	

Method

Cover the veal with 1 litre of stock in your saucepan, bring to the boil, skim, cover and simmer for 30 minutes. Drop in the potatoes, onions, celery and parsley stalks, cover again and simmer for 30 minutes more. Take out the veal and cut it in a small dice. Return it to the saucepan, bring soup back to heat, season to your taste, skim and serve in large hot soup plates, garnished with chopped parsley.

Lamb Soup with Parsley

Qengj Supë Me Majdanoz

Ingredients *(Serves 4)*

500g	lean leg of lamb, cut in small cubes	1 tbsp	flour +
		1 tbsp	butter, for a roux
1	bunch of scallions, finely chopped	2	hard-boiled eggs, diced
			Natural yogurt
1	bunch of parsley, finely chopped		A little extra butter
			Salt

Method

Pour 1 litre of water over the lamb in your saucepan, add half a teaspoon of salt and bring to the boil. Cover and simmer for 30 minutes. Meanwhile, lightly fry the scallions and parsley in a little butter and, when the 30 minutes are up, add them to the soup and simmer, covered, for another 30 minutes. Skim and serve in warm bowls with the diced egg spooned in and a dollop of yogurt on top.

Fresh Water Fish Soup

Ujë Det Supë

We had a family cottage on the shores of
Lough Corrib in the West of Ireland where we
fished in the summer and shot wild duck in
the winter. The lake, famous for mayfly fishing
in early June, provided plenty of trout; plenty of
pike and perch, too. I made soups there much
like this one – yogurt, an unthinkable exotic in
those days – excluded.

Ingredients *(Serves 4)*

500g	carp fillet, skinned and cut in bite-sized chunks	2	shallots, finely chopped
500g	trout fillet, skinned and cut in bite-sized chunks	1	bunch of parsley stalks, finely chopped
500g	pike fillet, skinned and cut in bite-sized chunks	2 tsp	butter
1 litre	fish stock		Natural yogurt
			Chopped parsley

Method

Sweat the chopped shallots and parsley stalks in the butter and a little
water in a small covered saucepan for 5 minutes, agitating it from time
to time. Empty this into your large saucepan with any juice that
remains. Add the fish and parsley stalks, pour on the stock, bring it to
the boil and simmer, uncovered, for 12 minutes. Skim and season to
your taste. Remove the fish with a slotted spoon and divide it equally
between 4 warm soup plates. Ladle on the soup and serve garnished
with chopped parsley and a flash of yogurt.

Vegetable Soup

Lentil Soup *Vospov Abour*

Ingredients *(Serves 6)*

70g	rinsed red lentils	2 tbsp	vegetable oil
1.5	litres chicken stock	1 tbsp	dried mint
1	medium onion, diced	20g	fine egg noodles
2 tbsp	butter		Salt and pepper

Method

In your large saucepan sauté the onion in the oil and butter until soft but not coloured. Then stir in the dried mint. Pour on the chicken stock and bring to the boil. Stir in the lentils, cover and simmer for 30 minutes, then season to your taste. Add the egg noodles and simmer for 10 minutes more. Skim and serve in warm bowls.

Vegetable Soup *Panjareghen Abour*

Ingredients *(Serves 4)*

1	medium potato, diced	1	small green pepper, de-seeded and diced
1	medium onion, diced		
2	celery stalks, diced	1	white turnip, diced
10	green beans, cut in 2cm pieces	500 ml	chicken stock
		200 ml	plain tomato juice
2	carrots, diced		Salt and pepper

Method

Pour the chicken stock and tomato juice into your saucepan, bring to the boil and add in all the vegetables. Simmer, covered, for 30 minutes. Skim and serve in warm bowls.

Hot Yogurt Soup 1 *Dak Tahnabour*

Ingredients *(Serves 8)*

100g	inner celery stalks, finely chopped	1	large onion, finely chopped
100g	bulgur*	3 tbsp	butter
1 litre	yogurt	1 tbsp	of vegetable oil
1	egg	1 dsp	dried mint
2 tbsp	flour	Celery salt	

Method

Pour 1 litre of water into your large saucepan, bring to the boil, stir in the bulgur and simmer gently, covered, for 1 hour or until all the water is absorbed. Put the bulgur aside in a bowl. In the rinsed saucepan, sauté the onion and the celery in the butter until the onion begins to brown. In your liquidiser, blend in batches, the egg, mint, flour and yogurt with 500ml water and stir it well into the bowl of soaked bulgur. Pour this mixture into the saucepan on the flame.

Bring to the boil, stirring all the time, and allow it to simmer, uncovered, to prevent curdling.** Blend again with your hand blender to get rid of the porridge texture. Season to your taste and serve at table, ladled from a tureen on to large soup plates.

*   *Also known as cracked or hulled wheat, it acts as a thickening agent.*

**   *Yogurt curdles when cooked covered.*

For palates unused to the flavour of this soup, diluting it by one third with chicken stock helps.

Cold Yogurt Soup *Bagh Tahnabour*

This simple soup is remarkably refreshing in very hot weather.

Ingredients *(Serves 4)*

125g	bulgur	1 tsp	salt
750ml	yogurt	Fresh mint, finely chopped	

Method

Pour 1 litre of water into your large saucepan, bring to the boil, stir in the bulgur and simmer, covered, for 1 hour or until the water is absorbed. Take it off the flame and allow to cool. Whisk the yogurt and stir it into the soaked bulgur with the salt. Dilute with a little water and then hand-blend to the consistency you want. Chill overnight and serve garnished with the chopped mint.

Hot Yogurt Soup 2 *Madzoon Abour*

Ingredients *(Serves 6)*

		½ tsp	dried mint
1 litre	natural yogurt	25g	flour
125g	bulgur	1	egg
1	large onion, finely	125g	spinach leaves, chopped
	chopped	1 tsp	salt

Method

Pour 1 litre of water into your large saucepan, bring to the boil, stir in the bulgur and simmer until it has almost absorbed the water (about 1 hour). Stir in the spinach, dried mint and salt and cook for 10 minutes more. Blend the flour and egg in 150ml of water and then blend the yogurt into this with your hand blender or in batches in your liquidiser. Strain it all into a large bowl. Melt the butter in your frying pan and sauté the chopped onion until it begins to turn colour. Stir the yogurt mixture on to the spinach mixture in the uncovered saucepan, add the onion, dried mint and salt, and bring it to the boil. Simmer gently for 5 minutes. Blend it once again to the texture you want and serve the soup in warm bowls garnished with a fresh mint leaf.

Chickpea Soup *Siserr Abour*

Ingredients *(Serves 6/8)*

420g	can of chickpeas, drained	225g	barley
225g	yellow split peas	2 tbsp	vegetable fat
2	small onions, finely	1 tsp	salt
	chopped		Cayenne and black pepper

Method

In your saucepan pour 1.5 litres of water over the barley, split peas and half of the chopped onion and bring to the boil. Simmer, covered, for 1 hour, stirring from time to time. Skim. Meanwhile sauté the remaining onions in the vegetable oil on a frying pan until they begin to brown. Pour these into the saucepan with the drained chickpeas. Season to your taste, bring it back up to heat and blend with your hand blender. Serve in large bowls, with pitta bread.

Chicken Soup *Hav Abour*

Ingredients *(Serves 6/8)*

1	small free-range chicken with giblets	300g	egg noodles
		1.5	litres chicken stock
2	medium onions, diced		Salt and white pepper
125g	long-grained rice		

Method

Sauté the onions in oil in your large saucepan until soft but not coloured. Put in the chicken, the giblets and the rice, pour on the stock and bring it to the boil. Skim and simmer, covered, for 60 minutes and remove the chicken and giblets. Stir in the egg noodles and simmer until tender (about 10 minutes). Meanwhile, dispose of the gizzard and chicken skin, take the meat off the bones and carcass, and cut it in a large dice. Chop up the liver and drop the lot back into the saucepan. This hefty soup, seasoned to your taste, should be served in large soup plates, with well-buttered chunks of crispy bread on the side.

Beetroot Soup *Garmeer Dag Abour*

The first time I had this soup was in an Armenian restaurant in London very many years ago. It was served with warm pitta bread spread with a thick chickpea paste (hummus), neither of which I had tasted before. It was fantastic then, still is, and it goes extremely well with many Middle Eastern soups.

Ingredients *(Serves 4)*

3	medium beetroots, trimmed and diced	Juice of half a lemon
125g	barley	Yogurt
125g	split peas	Salt

Method
Put the diced beetroots, barley, split peas and lemon juice into your large saucepan, pour on 1 litre of water and bring it to the boil. Skim, and simmer, covered, for 65 minutes or until the beet is soft. Blend well with your hand blender or in batches in your liquidiser. Season to your taste and serve in warm bowls with a dollop of yogurt on top.

Armenian Soup *Haigagan Abour*

Ingredients *(Serves 4)*

750ml	chicken stock	2tsp	lemon juice
100g	vermicelli	Salt	
1	egg, beaten		

Method

Pour the stock into your large saucepan and bring to the boil. Add the vermicelli and salt to your taste. Simmer for 10 minutes. Meanwhile, beat the egg and lemon juice with 4 tablespoons of water and, when the soup is ready, spoon 4 tablespoons of hot soup into the egg mixture. This in turn is poured in a thin stream into the not-quite-simmering soup, stirring all the time to prevent curdling. Serve immediately in warm bowls.

Meatball Soup *Blor Kufta Abour*

Ingredients *(Serves 4/6)*

500g	minced beef	2 tbsp	tomato paste
1	medium onion, finely chopped	1 litre	chicken stock
50g	cooked bulgur	Salt	

Method

Mix the onion, bulgur, minced beef and salt to your taste in your liquidiser or food processor, using the non-cutting blade. Form the mixture into cherry-sized balls in your floured hands and chill for an hour or so. Pour the stock into your saucepan with the tomato paste. Add the meatballs. Bring to the boil and simmer, uncovered, until the meatballs rise to the surface. Serve in warm, deep soup plates.

Sturgeon Soup

I got this recipe from a scientist who enjoyed the pleasures of dining on sturgeon on board an oil exploration vessel in the Caspian Sea. Although it is illegal to catch sturgeon in the Caspian, it has been known for illegal nets with sturgeon in them to foul the paravanes carrying the echo devices which are trailed on cables 5km long at a depth of about 7 metres. These fish are cut up on board, salted and dried in the sun on deck. This recipe uses the freshly caught parts which are not used in the drying process. The dried fish is used much like salt cod in the recipe for Basque Cod Soup (see page 173).

Ingredients (Serves 8)

2kg	sturgeon bones and head, gills removed, all chopped	8	trimmed slices of wholemeal bread
2	onions, diced		Juice of a whole lemon
2	carrots. diced		Natural yogurt
1	celery heart, diced		Dill, chopped
75g	butter		Salt and white pepper

Method

Pour 2 litres of cold water on to the sturgeon pieces in your large saucepan and bring it to the boil. Simmer uncovered for 20 minutes and strain out the solids. Sweat the diced onion, celery and carrot in the butter and a little water in a medium saucepan, covered, for 5 minutes, agitating it from time to time. Pour the stock back into the large saucepan and bring it to the boil. Skim and pour in the sweated vegetables with their juices and the lemon juice. Simmer for 10 minutes and season to your taste. Put a tablespoon of yogurt on to each slice of wholemeal bread and sprinkle chopped dill on top. Ladle the soup on to each warm soup plate and serve quickly with the garnished bread on top. Alternatively serve with the soup poured on to the bread.

Armenia

Beef Soup with Crispy Vegetables

Beef Soup with Crispy Vegetables
Ochsenfleischsuppe mit Knuspriggemüse

Austria (map, Vienna, AUSTRIA)

Ingredients *(Serves 4/6)*

1	celery stalk, finely chopped	75g	peas
1	medium carrot, in a small dice	1 litre	beef stock
1	stalk of Kohlrabi, in a small dice (see p. 195)	6	rashers of streaky bacon, fried to a crisp
8	Brussels sprouts, par-boiled and thinly sliced	4	slices of white bread, crusts removed
12	green beans, sliced small		Parmesan cheese, grated
			Salt and pepper
			Parsley stalks, finely chopped

Method

Stir all the vegetables into boiling salted water in your saucepan and cook for 6 to 8 minutes. Remove the vegetables with a slotted spoon, rinse in cold water and put aside in a bowl of cold water. Butter the bread, cut it into large croutons, sprinkle with Parmesan and brown under the grill. Chop up the crispy bacon and put it aside. Empty the saucepan of the vegetable water, pour in the beef stock and bring to the boil. Stir the cold vegetables into the stock. Allow to simmer for 2 minutes more and season to your taste. Ladle into heated soup plates over the crispy bacon. Serve with the croutons on top.

Cabbage Soup *Kohlsuppe*

Ingredients *(Serves 5)*

500ml	vegetable stock	1 tbsp	flour
1	medium cabbage, trimmed and shredded in thin ribbons	2 tbsp	beef dripping
		8	frankfurters

Method

Sweat the cabbage in 125ml of water in your large saucepan, covered, for about 15 minutes, checking the water from time to time. Take out the cabbage and remaining water and put it aside. Brown the flour in the dripping. Stir in the stock and cabbage water slowly at first, bring to the boil and simmer, covered, stirring from time to time for 45 minutes. Boil the frankfurters* separately, slice them hot and add them to the soup before serving in hot soup plates.

* *Pierced frankfurters cook easily in your microwave oven.*

Bread Soup *Panadlsuppe*

Ingredients *(Serves 4)*

6	slices of stale white bread, cut in squares	125ml	cream
			Chives, chopped
1 litre	beef consommé		Butter
1	egg yolk		Salt and white pepper

Method

Cover the bread in your saucepan with the consommé, bring to the boil, stir with a whisk until the bread has absorbed the stock and season it to your taste. Blend the egg yolk into the cream and gradually stir this into the soup just below boiling point. Serve immediately in warm bowls, garnished with the chives and a pat of butter on top.

Liver Dumpling Soup *Leberknödelsuppe*

This hearty soup is a classic in the sense that it became part of The Third Man *in the movie of that name set in Vienna. Not Harry Lime, nor the Orson Wells who played the part, but Orson, the real life gourmand, who increased his girth by a third before he went to that great dining room in the sky. I am sure he slurped this soup in his day.*

Ingredients *(Serves 4)*

SOUP
450ml beef stock
Parsley, chopped, to garnish
Salt

DUMPLINGS
8   slices of white bread, cut
        in squares
2 tbsp dried breadcrumbs

350ml   warm milk
1   medium onion, finely
        chopped
400g   beef liver, ground
1   egg
2 tbsp parsley, chopped
2   pinches dried marjoram
White pepper (shake of)
Butter

Method

To make the dumplings. First put the bread into a large bowl, sprinkle it with salt and pour on the warm milk. Cover the bowl and let it stand for an hour. Meanwhile, sauté the onion in some butter in a frying pan until soft but not coloured, adding the chopped parsley for the last few minutes of the operation. When cool, stir this with the ground liver, egg, marjoram and pepper into the soaked bread bowl. Add the dried breadcrumbs and blend well with your hand blender or in batches in the liquidiser. With floured hands, shape into 8 cherry-sized* dumplings and chill them for about an hour. Bring 1 litre of salted water to the boil in your saucepan, lower it to a gentle simmer, drop in the dumplings with a slotted spoon and cook, uncovered, until they rise to the surface. Remove and keep warm.

To make the soup. Pour away the dumpling water and pour on the beef stock, bring to the boil, stir in the milk and bring *just* to the boil. To serve, put 2 dumplings into each warm soup plate, ladle on the soup and garnish with chopped parsley.

* *Dumplings expand to double their size .*

Goulash Soup *Goulashsuppe*

Ingredients *(Serves 5)*

250g	leg of beef, minced	2 tbsp	beef dripping
3	waxy potatoes, cooked, peeled and cubed	1 tbsp	paprika
		$^1/_2$ tsp	caraway seeds
4	medium onions, sliced	2	cloves of garlic, crushed
2 tbsp	tomato purée	1 litre	water
		Salt	

Method

Brown the onions with the dripping in your large saucepan, add the mince and brown it too. Drop in all the other ingredients except the potatoes. Cover with water and bring to the boil. Skim and simmer for 30 minutes. Add the potatoes, season to your taste and simmer for a further 10 minutes. Allow to cool and blend well in batches in your liquidiser or food processor. Pour the soup back into the saucepan, remove any fat from the surface and bring it to serving temperature. Serve in warm bowls.

Vegetable Soup *Gemüsesuppe*

Ingredients *(Serves 4)*

2	medium onions, diced	1	medium waxy potato, diced
1	medium carrot, diced		
1	medium white turnip, diced	2 tbsp	butter
			Croutons
2	celery stalks, sliced thinly		Salt and pepper
1 litre	vegetable stock		

Method

Sauté the diced onion, carrot, turnip and celery in the butter in your saucepan until the onion softens but does not colour. Pour on the stock, add the diced potato and bring to the boil. Season and simmer, covered, for 30 minutes. Skim and serve in warm bowls with croutons.

Cream of Endive Soup

Potage Crème d'endives

'Chicory Chick, Chala, Chala, Chick à la Gumbo' were the opening words of a popular song I used to hear years ago. It was a non-sense song, of course, but I often wondered if it had been composed by a chef. Chicory is another name for endive and gumbo another name for okra, used in some soups and stews. Well, there's chicory in this one and take a look at Sarajevo Soup, p. 41

Ingredients *(Serves 4)*

2	endives, chopped	500ml	chicken stock
1	onion, chopped	250ml	cream
1	clove of garlic, chopped		Chives, chopped
2 tbsp	butter		Salt and white pepper
2	large potatoes, peeled and cubed		

Method

Sauté the onion and garlic with the butter in your large saucepan until they soften but do not colour. Add the endives, potatoes and stock. Bring to the boil and skim. Season to your taste, cover and simmer for 30 minutes. Allow to cool and blend well with your hand blender or in batches in your liquidiser. Return this to the saucepan, stir in the cream, bring the soup back to heat and serve in warm bowls, garnished with the chopped chives on top.

Belgium

Belgian Leek Soup

Belgian Leek Soup *Potage Crème de Poireaux*

Ingredients *(Serves 8)*

4	large leeks, chopped coarsely, including about 4 cm of the green parts	I	cup dry white wine
		250ml	cream
		$^1/_2$ tsp	nutmeg
125g	diced bacon	Grated Provolone (piccante) cheese	
2	celery stalks, finely diced		
150g	plain flour +	Croutons	
150g	butter, for a roux	Salt and white pepper	
I litre	chicken stock		

Method

In a medium covered saucepan, sweat the leeks in 100g butter and some water for about 10 minutes. In your large saucepan fry the diced bacon and celery until they begin to brown. Put in the leeks and nutmeg. Pour on the stock, wine and a litre of water, and bring to the boil. Skim and simmer, covered, for 30 minutes. Stir in the roux and when the soup thickens add the cream. Season to your taste and serve in warm bowls with croutons and grated cheese on the side.

Crab Soup *Potage Purée de Crabes*

Ingredients *(Serves 5)*

250g	white crabmeat	2 tsp	Worcestershire sauce
I litre	fish stock	I tbsp	(heaped) cornflour
420g	can of diced tomatoes	Chopped parsley	
2	thin leeks, sliced finely	Salt and pepper	
I	bottle of ale		

Method

Bring the ale to the boil in your large saucepan to get rid of the alcohol. Pour in the fish stock and add the crabmeat, tomatoes and leeks. Season to your taste, spoon in the Worcestershire sauce and simmer for 10 minutes. Mix the cornflour in some cold water, add to the soup and, when it thickens, serve it in warm bowls garnished with chopped parsley.

Chicken Soup with Okra

Kokoshka Supa I Okra

Ingredients *(Serves 5/6)*

1 litre	chicken stock	20g	long-grained rice, cooked
2	chicken breasts, diced	2	egg yolks, whipped
1	medium carrot, diced	3 tbsp	sour cream
100g	diced celeriac	A squeeze of lemon juice	
50g	okra, cooked	Salt	

Method

In your large saucepan bring the chicken stock to the boil, drop in the carrot, diced chicken and celeriac. Simmer, skim and cook, covered, for 15 minutes. Bring it up to simmer again and, stirring well with a Paris whisk, pour in the egg yolk in a thin stream. Season to your taste, then add the rice and okra. Just before serving, stir in the cream with a squeeze of lemon.

Sarajevo Soup

Ingredients *(Serves 4/5)*

125g	veal, diced	2	egg yolks
1 litre	veal stock	150ml	sour cream
25g	butter		Salt
50g	diced carrots		Black pepper
50g	diced onions		Lemon juice
50g	fresh okra pods		Chopped parsley

Method

Sauté the diced veal and vegetables in butter in your medium saucepan until the onion softens, but does not brown. Stir in the flour with a wooden spoon, making sure it absorbs the butter. Pour on the veal stock, bring to the boil and, when it thickens slightly, skim off the impurities. Season to your taste, add the okra, cover and simmer for 20 minutes. Mix the egg yolks and sour cream in a bowl, stir into the simmering soup and turn off the flame immediately to avoid curdling. Serve on warm soup plates with a squeeze of lemon juice.

Pasta Crumb Soup *Tarhana*

Ingredients *(Serves 6)*

SOUP

1.5 litres of beef stock
50g   plain flour +
50g   butter, for a roux
2   tomatoes, skinned, de-
       seeded and chopped
White pepper
Paprika

PASTA

2   eggs
200g   plain flour
1 tbsp tomato paste
1 tsp salt

Method

Make the pasta four days ahead of serving the soup. Mix a stiff dough with the eggs, tomato paste and the flour, then let it rest, covered, for 4 days. At the end of this period, chop half the dough★ into small portions and grind each carefully in your liquidiser to a crumb consistency. Dry them off in your microwave oven on kitchen paper, in short bursts. Use your own judgment … the consistency should not be hard.
To make the soup. Pour the stock into your medium saucepan, bring to the boil, simmer and season with salt to your taste. In your small saucepan make the roux and stir in 4 ladles of the hot stock until it thickens well. Put this aside. Stir the pasta crumbs and chopped tomatoes into the stock, simmer for 10 minutes and then stir in the thickened stock. When that is absorbed, serve on soup plates with the paprika sprinkled on top.

★ *You can roll out the unused pasta and cut it in narrow strips for use as a type of tagliatelle.*

More bread is eaten with food in Bulgaria than any other country in the Balkans. Bread goes well with all the soups I describe here, especially when spread with butter or dipped in virgin olive oil.

Tomato Soup *Domatene Cyna*

Ingredients *(Serves 6/8)*

SOUP

I large	onion, diced
4	cloves garlic, minced
3 tbsp	olive oil
2 × 420g	cans of diced tomatoes
I litre	vegetable stock
½ tsp	chilli powder
2 tbsp	flour
I tsp	salt
I tsp	black pepper

DUMPLINGS

2tbsp	butter
2	eggs, separated
100g	polenta
60g	boiling water
120g	flour
I tsp	salt

Method

To make the dumplings. Put the egg yolks, butter, salt, polenta and flour into your blender, pour on the boiling water in a thin stream and blend it to a paste. Whip the egg whites to a soft peak and in a separate bowl fold into the dumpling paste. Shape the dumplings to the size of a cherries in your floured hands.

To make the soup. Sauté the onion and garlic with the olive oil in your large saucepan until soft but not coloured. Stir in the flour and allow it to colour to a light brown. Pour on the stock a little at a time, stirring until you have a sauce. At this point, pour on the remaining stock, add the tomatoes and bring the soup to the boil. Put in the rest of the ingredients and simmer, covered, for 30 minutes, stirring from time to time. Blend the soup with your hand blender or in batches in your liquidiser. Bring the soup back up to a simmer, drop in the dumplings and, when they rise to the surface, the soup is ready. Serve at table from a tureen, ladled onto large warmed soup plates.

Bulgaria

43

Tripe Soup

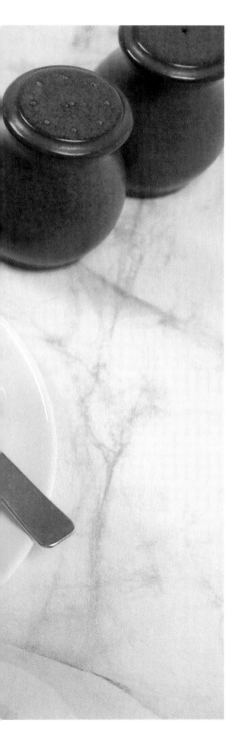

Tripe Soup
Chkembe Tchorba

Ingredients (Serves 4/5)

375g	tripe, cooked and cut in thin strips
750ml	beef stock
1	onion, finely chopped
1	red pepper, cut in thin strips
3 tbsp	butter
2 tbsp	flour
1	bay leaf
125g	tomato paste
1	clove of garlic, finely chopped
½ tsp	dried marjoram
200g	grated Kaskaval* cheese
Chopped parsley	
Salt	

Method

Sweat the onion and red pepper with the butter and a little water in your medium saucepan until soft, about 10 minutes. Pour these with juices into your large saucepan and stir in the flour. When it is blended, pour on the stock with the tomato paste, bay leaf, red pepper and marjoram and bring to the boil. Season to your taste, stir in the tripe and simmer gently, loosely covered, for 30 minutes. Skim and serve in heated bowls with a mixture of the garlic, cheese and parsley sprinkled on top.

* *Kaskaval is a mild, milky cheese made from ewes' milk. Gouda or Edam are reasonable substitutes if you cannot find Kaskaval.*

Bulgaria

Chilled Cucumber Soup

Nastinka Krastavica Cyna

Ingredients *(Serves 4)*

I	medium cucumber, pared, de-seeded and chopped	250ml	sour cream
I	large clove of garlic, finely chopped	2 tbsp	olive oil
175g	walnuts, chopped		Fresh dill, chopped
500ml	vegetable stock chilled		Salt and white pepper (level tsp mixed)

Method

In a bowl, make up a marinade of the garlic, dill, walnuts, olive oil and the salt and pepper. Mix in the chopped cucumber. Refrigerate for 5 hours. Purée this in your liquidiser. Stir in the cream just before serving and pour the soup over 2 ice cubes in each bowl. Garnish with chopped dill.

Chilled Curd Soup *Tarator*

Ingredients *(Serves 4)*

SOUP		DRIED CURD	
3 tbsp	dried curd	I	small red pepper
2 tbsp	tomato paste	2 tbsp	curd
3	cloves of garlic, crushed	2 tbsp	yogurt
I	tbsp butter	I tbsp	flour
I	tsp dried mint	I	tomato, de-seeded
500ml	milk	I	small onion, chopped
I tsp	rennet*	I tsp	yeast
		Salt	

Method

Make the curd 10 days in advance. Put all the curd ingredients into a bowl and blend them with your hand blender or in your liquidiser.

* An agent for separating milk into curd and whey in cheese making.

Cover the bowl with a cloth and put it in a cool place where it will dry and ferment. In 10 days it will be ready for use. You can store it in your fridge for up to 10 days.

To make the soup. Put the rennet into 500ml of milk in a bowl and let it stand until it separates, then pour it through a strainer to get rid of the whey. Put the curd into a bowl with 250ml cold water and allow stand for 10 minutes. Melt the butter in your large saucepan, sauté the garlic in it until it softens but does not colour. Stir in the tomato paste, pour on 600ml of water and bring to the boil. Pour on the curd mixture and simmer for about 12 minutes, stirring all the time. Serve in warm bowls with dried mint sprinkled on top.

Yoghurt Soup *Yoghurt Cyna*

Ingredients *(Serves 6)*

250g	natural yogurt	1	egg yolk
1.5	litres chicken stock	1/2 tsp	cayenne pepper
70g	cooked rice	Dried mint	
50g	plain flour +	Salt	
60g	butter		

Method

Melt the butter in your large saucepan, stir in the flour and cook until it begins to brown. Stir in a little of the stock at first and then add the rest, stirring from time to time. Bring to the boil. Drop in the rice and gently simmer, uncovered, for 10 minutes. Meanwhile, lightly whisk the egg yolk into the yogurt in a bowl. Then gradually stir this into the soup in a thin stream. Skim and season to your taste. Brown a half teaspoon of cayenne pepper in a little butter and stir this into the soup. Serve in warm bowls sprinkled with dried mint.

Bulgarian Meatball Soup *Meatball Cyna*

Ingredients *(Serves 4)*

MEATBALLS		SOUP	
200g	minced lean beef	I litre	beef stock
I	small onion, minced	100g	long-grained rice
I tsp	thyme	I	clove garlic, crushed
2	small eggs, beaten	2tbsp	fresh dill
I tsp	salt		Yogurt
Black pepper			Lemon juice

Method

To make the meatballs. Mix the beef, onion, thyme, eggs, salt and pepper in a bowl. Make the mix into walnut-sized meatballs in your floured hands and put aside.

To make the soup. Bring the stock up to boiling point in your saucepan, drop in the meatballs, garlic and rice, and simmer, covered, for 30 minutes. Add the dill, season and add lemon juice to your taste. Serve at table from a tureen with a dollop of yogurt in each bowl of soup.

Bean Soup *Bob Cyna*

Ingredients *(Serves 6)*

		50g	tomato paste
420g	can of white beans, with their juice	I litre	vegetable stock
		2	green peppers, diced
2	large carrots, diced		Parsley, chopped
5	sticks celery, finely sliced		Fresh mint leaves
I	large onion, diced		Cream
Vegetable oil			Salt

Method

Sauté the vegetables in some oil in your large saucepan until the onion is soft but not coloured. Pour on the stock and bring to the boil. Add the tomato paste and simmer, covered, for 20 minutes. Season to your taste, stir in the beans with their juice, drop in 2 or 3 mint leaves; if you like a strong flavour, add a few more mint leaves. Skim and serve in warm bowls with a sprinkle of cream on top.

Lamb Soup *Janje Juha*

Ingredients *(Serves 6)*

400g	lean lamb meat, cut in cubes
1	large onion, chopped
1	large carrot, cut in cubes
150g	Swede turnip, cut in cubes
2	cloves garlic, crushed
2	raw egg yolks
100ml	smetana (see p. 194)
65g	cooked rice
65g	Savoy cabbage, cut in thin ribbons
1	bay leaf
1 tbsp	mixed spices
6	peppercorns
Juice of a lemon	
Chopped parsley	
Salt	
Vegetable oil	

Method

Brown the meat all over with a little vegetable oil in your large saucepan. Take it off the flame and pour away the oil. Return it to the flame and pour on 1.5 litres of boiling water; then simmer, covered, for 30 minutes. At the same time, cook the cabbage, covered, in your medium saucepan. Strain the cabbage and put aside. Add the rest of the vegetables, the bay leaf, peppercorns and mixed spice to the stock and bring it to boiling point. Skim and simmer, covered, for a further 35 minutes. Season to your taste. To avoid curdling at the next stage, make sure the soup is just below boiling point. Mix the egg yolks, smetana and lemon juice in a bowl and stir them into the soup gradually. When it has thickened, drop in the rice and cabbage. Serve this hearty soup in large bowls, garnished with chopped parsley.

Croatia

49

Potato Soup

Potato Soup from Zagorje*

Krumpir-Juha Zagorje

Ingredients *(Serves 5)*

700g	potatoes, peeled and cubed	1 tsp	(heaped) sweet paprika
100g	smoked rashers of bacon, chopped	1	bay leaf
		1 tbsp	mixed spices
50g	butter	Small	bunch fresh marjoram, chopped
2	cloves garlic, chopped		
1	medium onion, chopped	Parsley, chopped	
200ml	smetana (see p. 194)	Salt	
50g	flour	Black pepper	

Method

Melt the butter in your medium saucepan and sauté the bacon and onion until the onion is soft but not browned. Sprinkle it with the paprika. Pour off the butter into a small saucepan and make a roux with the flour. Pour on 1.25 litres of water and stir in the potatoes, mixed spices, garlic and bay leaf. Bring to the boil, skim and simmer, covered, for 30 minutes. Take off the flame and allow to cool, removing the bay leaf with a slotted spoon. Purée the soup in batches in your food processor or liquidiser, then pour it back into the saucepan. Bring to boiling point, season to your taste, stir in the roux and, when it thickens, stir in the smetana and marjoram and simmer for 2 minutes. Serve immediately, garnished with chopped parsley.

* *A county north of Zagreb.*

Mushroom Soup with Buckwheat
Gljiva Juha Sa Heljda

Ingredients *(Serves 5)*

1	litre vegetable stock	1 tbsp	plain flour
200g	field mushrooms, sliced	1	bay leaf
10g	dried mushrooms	100ml	vegetable oil
50g	buckwheat	Red wine vinegar	
1	small onion, chopped	Salt	
2	cloves garlic, chopped	Black pepper	
50ml	sour cream	Chopped parsley for garnish	

Method

Make a smooth paste with the flour and sour cream. Soak the dried mushrooms in boiled water for 20 minutes. Put the sliced field mushrooms into a small saucepan with 2 tablespoons of water and sweat them, covered, on a medium flame for about 3 minutes. Put aside. Sauté the onion and garlic in the vegetable oil in your medium saucepan until they become soft but not coloured. Then pour off the oil. Pour on the vegetable stock, the cooked field mushrooms and the dried mushrooms with their liquids, the buckwheat and the bay leaf. Bring to the boil, skim and simmer gently, covered, for 20 minutes. Season to your taste. Stir in the sour cream paste with a Paris whisk and, when the soup thickens, add red wine vinegar to your taste. Serve on warm soup plates, garnished with chopped parsley.

Cream of Broccoli Soup
Vrchol Čeho Broccolli Polévka

Ingredients (Serves 6)

2	heads of broccoli florets, with their stalks peeled and sliced*	500ml	cream
		250g	smoked streaky rashers of bacon, rinds on
2	large carrots, sliced	150g	butter +
4	celery stalks, strings removed and sliced	150g	plain flour, for a roux
1 litre	vegetable stock	Salt	
		Black pepper	

Method

Fry the rashers whole in your large saucepan until crispy all over. Remove with a slotted spoon and put aside on kitchen paper. Drop the chopped carrot and celery into the bacon fat and sauté for about 5 minutes. Pour off the fat through a strainer and dry the vegetables on kitchen paper. Return them to the saucepan with the broccoli florets and sliced stalks, pour on the stock and bring to boiling point. Skim and simmer, covered, for 30 minutes. While this is happening, make the roux and then put it aside. Crush the crispy bacon with a rolling pin. Allow the soup to cool and purée it in batches in your food processor or in the saucepan with a hand blender. Put the saucepan back on the flame and bring the soup to boiling point. Stir in the roux with a Paris whisk and when the soup thickens, turn off the flame and stir in the cream. Serve on warm soup plates with the crushed crispy bacon sprinkled on top.

*   The stalk is the thick one below the head which is some-times removed in the shop. This is a mistake because it has excellent flavour. It is important to shave off the skin of the stalk, which can taste bitter.

53

Potato Soup *Bramborová Polévka*

Ingredients *(Serves 5)*

2	medium potatoes, chopped	I pinch	of caraway seed
I	large carrot, chopped	I pinch	of allspice
150g	mushrooms, sliced	2 tbsp	plain flour +
I	inner celery stalk, chopped	2 tbsp	butter, for a roux
		Cream for garnish	
I	medium onion, chopped	Salt	
		Black pepper	

Method

Pour a litre of water into your large saucepan and bring to the boil. Drop in all the vegetables, bring back to the boil and skim. Simmer, covered, for 35 minutes. Then stir in the caraway seed and the allspice and simmer for a further 5 minutes. Turn off the flame and season to your taste. When the soup cools, purée it in your food processor or in the saucepan with your hand blender. Return it to the flame and bring back to boiling point. Stir in the roux with a Paris whisk and, when the soup thickens, serve it on warm soup plates with a flash of cream on top.

Cabbage Soup with Frankfurters

Zelná Polévka S Párke

Ingredients *(Serves 5)*

I	small white cabbage, chopped	4	cooked frankfurters, thinly sliced
I litre	beef stock	2 tbsp	flour
I	large waxy potato, cooked and cut in a small dice	2 tbsp	lard
		Chopped parsley	
I	large onion, diced	Salt and black pepper	

Method

Sauté the chopped cabbage and the onion in the lard in the bottom of

Cabbage Soup with Frankfurters

your medium saucepan, stirring with a wooden spoon, until they are soft but not coloured. Pour the melted lard into your small saucepan and put aside. Add the stock to the vegetables and bring to the boil. Skim and simmer, covered, for 20 minutes. Heat the lard again, stir in the flour and make a roux. Season to your taste. Sir in the roux and, when the soup thickens, add the diced potatoes and sliced frankfurters. If the soup is too thick, pour in a little boiling water until you get the consistency you like. Serve in warm bowls, garnished with the chopped parsley.

Chervil Soup with Eggs

Chervil Soup with Eggs

Hæge Om Suppe Hos Æggene

DENMARK
Copenhagen

Ingredients *(Serves 6)*

1.5 litres	vegetable stock
3	medium carrots, sliced
2	small leeks, chopped
3 tbsp	butter +
3 tbsp	flour, for a roux
6	small eggs, poached
150g	chervil, chopped

Salt and pepper

Method

Bring the stock to the boil in your large saucepan, add the carrots, leeks and chervil, skim and season to your taste and simmer, covered, for 25 minutes. Allow to cool. Pour the soup through a sieve, blend the carrots, leeks and chervil in your liquidiser or food processor in batches and then return them to the saucepan with the soup. Bring back to the boil. Make a roux with the flour and butter and stir it into the soup with a Paris whisk. When it thickens, ladle it into warm bowls over a poached egg.

Denmark

Pea Soup *Pea Suppe*

Ingredients *(Serves 5)*

250g	yellow split peas	4	medium leeks, chopped
500g	lean bacon	2	medium onions, chopped
250g	sausages	50g	butter
3	medium carrots, chopped	½ tsp	dried thyme
150g	celeriac, shredded	Salt and pepper	

Method

Pour boiling water on the split peas and leave to soak overnight. In your large saucepan, sauté the onions and leeks with the butter until soft but not coloured. Add the bacon, pour on the water and bring it to the boil. Simmer for 20 minutes. Add the strained split peas, thyme and carrots and simmer for 30 minutes, stirring from time to time. Pierce the sausages and cook them in the soup for 10 more minutes. Take out the bacon and sausages and keep them warm. Skim the soup and blend well with a hand blender or in batches in your liquidiser. Return this to the saucepan and season to your taste. Bring the soup to serving heat and serve in warm bowls at table with the sliced bacon and sausages on a platter and crusty, buttered bread on the side.

Fruit and Sago Soup *Frut Og Sago Suppe*

Ingredients *(Serves 5)*

200g	prunes, cut in four	65ml	water
100g	raisins	1	cinnamon stick
85g	sago +		

Method

Put the prunes, raisins and cinnamon stick into a medium saucepan, pour in 1 litre of water and bring to the boil. Simmer, covered, for 30 minutes. Meanwhile, cook the sago separately in water until it thickens. Remove the cinnamon stick from the soup, stir in the sago and cook for a few more minutes. Serve hot or chilled.

Creamy Morel Soup *Fløde Flere Suppe*

Ingredients *(Serves 8)*

125g	morels	2 tbsp	butter
250g	button mushrooms	1 tsp	allspice
1.5 litres	vegetable stock	250ml	full cream
60ml	Tawny Port	3 tbsp	chives, chopped

Method

Sweat the morels in half the butter in your medium, covered, saucepan and put aside with the buttery juice. Do the same with the button mushrooms. Purée half of both mushrooms, and dice the remaining morels and buttons. Bring the stock to the boil in a larger saucepan, add all the other ingredients – keep a tablespoon of chives for garnish! – plus the puréed and diced button mushrooms, morels and buttery juices. Simmer for 30 minutes. Then stir in the cream, simmer for another minute or so and serve* immediately in warm bowls garnished with chopped chives.

* *Skim off the butter at this stage if you like, but I prefer to leave it there for the pleasure of wiping the delicious residue of the soup and butter remaining in the bowl with bread, to finish with satisfaction.*

Apple Soup

Æble Suppe

Ingredients *(Serves 4)*

4	crisp, sweet apples, peeled and cubed	1 tbsp	curry powder
250ml	sweet white wine	250ml	cream
3	cloves	Sugar	
		Juice of half a lemon	

Method

Simmer all the ingredients except the cream and sugar in the white wine with 250ml water in your large saucepan for 15 minutes. Allow to cool, remove the cloves and blend the soup well in your liquidiser. Bring it back to the boil, add sugar to your taste and stir in the cream. Simmer for a minute or so. Serve hot if you like, though most fruit soups are better served cold.

Cheese Soup *Ost Suppe*

Ingredients *(Serves 4/5)*

4	whole scallions, finely chopped	500ml	chicken stock
2	carrots, diced	2 tbsp	butter +
2	celery stalks, sliced	2 tbsp	plain flour, for a roux
250g	soft cheese,* grated	1 tsp	paprika
500ml	milk	Salt and black pepper	

Method

Sweat the scallions with the butter in a small covered saucepan and, when soft, stir in the flour with a wooden spoon. Stir in half the milk and, when it thickens, put it aside. Pour the remainder of the milk and the chicken stock into your large saucepan with the carrots and celery and bring to the boil. Simmer, covered, for 20 minutes. Allow to cool and blend well in your liquidiser in batches. Transfer the scallion sauce to the large saucepan, put it back on the flame and stir in the blended soup. As it comes up to heat, carefully stir in the grated cheese. Season to your taste and allow the soup to bubble for a minute or so. Serve in bowls garnished with mild paprika.

*   *Use Danbo, Gouda or Edam cheese.*

Kidney Soup

Ingredients *(Serves 4)*

500g	beef kidneys	50g	plain flour +
1	onion, chopped	50g	butter, for a roux
1	carrot, chopped		Parsley, chopped
1 tbsp	mushroom ketchup		White pepper
1 litre	beef stock		Vegetable oil
1 tsp	celery salt		

Method

Remove the choke (fatty core) from the kidneys and cut them up into small pieces. Heat some oil in your saucepan, then fry the kidneys and onion until they begin to brown. Pour on the stock, drop in the carrot, celery salt and some parsley and bring to the boil. Skim, spoon in the mushroom ketchup and cook for 40 minutes, covered. Allow to cool. Take out the solids with a slotted spoon, cover them with a little of the soup in your liquidiser or food processor and blend in batches to a paste, before stirring back into the soup. Bring to boiling point, stir in the roux and, when it thickens, take it off the flame. Season to your taste and serve in warm bowls garnished with chopped parsley.

Tomato Soup

Ingredients *(Serves 6)*

2 × 420g	cans of tomatoes	1 tbsp	butter
1	carrot, chopped	100ml	cream, whipped
1	onion, chopped		Bouquet garni
2	celery stalks, chopped		Pepper and salt
750ml	chicken stock		A pinch of sugar
250ml	milk		

Method

Melt the butter in your saucepan, put in the carrots, onions and celery with a little water and sweat them, covered, over a medium flame

England

until the onion becomes translucent (about 10 minutes). Drop in the tomatoes and juice, the bouquet garni and the stock. Season to your taste, bring to the boil, skim and simmer for 45 minutes. Allow to cool and then remove the solids (dispose of the bouquet garni) with a slotted spoon. Put these into your food processor with some of the soup and the sugar, and blend well until they become smooth. Pour on the milk. Return to the saucepan and bring up to simmer. Serve with a dollop of whipped cream on top.

Oxtail Soup

Ingredients *(Serves 8)*

2.5kg	oxtail, cut at the joints	1	leek, white part only, chopped
2	large onions, chopped		
2	cloves of garlic, crushed	2	large potatoes, cooked and cubed
2	bay leaves		
125g	pearl barley	2 tbsp	vegetable oil
2 litres	water	1 tsp	dried thyme
2	celery stalks, chopped	Chopped parsley for garnish	
2	medium carrots, chopped	Salt and black pepper	

Method

Sauté the onions, celery, leeks and garlic in the oil until soft but not coloured in your large saucepan. Put in the oxtails, pour on 2 litres of water and bring to the boil. Add the carrots, barley, thyme, bay leaves and salt to your taste. Skim, cover and simmer for 2 hours. Remove the oxtails and the bay leaves. Skim all the fat from the soup. Drop in the cubed potatoes and a half teaspoon of black pepper. Simmer for ten minutes more and then blend the soup with a hand-whisk or in batches in your food processor. Season with salt to your taste. Serve in warm bowls garnished with chopped parsley. If you like, serve the oxtail with floury boiled potatoes as a main course.

Brown Windsor Soup

In the first half of the last century and the last half of the previous one, this soup was an absolute must on the luncheon menus of almost every hotel and boarding-house in the British Isles and probably the Empire too. I think, perhaps, Queen Victoria favoured it. The mind boggles at the lack of imagination of the then chefs and cooks. However, fortified with the sherry, it is very acceptable.

Ingredients *(Serves 6)*

1.5 litres	beef stock	2 tbsp	arrowroot
2	large carrots, chopped and diced		Chopped parsley for garnish
			Salt and white pepper

Method

Put aside 2 tablespoons of the cold stock. Bring the rest of it to the boil in your large saucepan, drop in the diced carrots and simmer for 30 minutes. Blend well with your hand blender. Mix the cold stock and the arrowroot in a small bowl and stir it into the simmering soup, which will thicken immediately.* Serve in warm soup plates, garnished with chopped parsley.

* *A glass of dry sherry poured in at this stage does the soup a power of good.*

Hodge Podge Soup with Dumplings

Ingredients *(Serves 6)*

SOUP

125g	frozen peas or broad beans	1	small can corned beef
2	onions, diced		Salt and pepper
2	carrots, diced		DUMPLINGS
500g	waxy potatoes, peeled, cooked and diced	110g	self-raising flour
1 litre	beef stock	50g	chopped suet
2 tbsp	vegetable oil	2 tbsp	water to make a soft dough
			Salt and pepper

Method

Make the dumplings an hour ahead in your food processor. Put all the ingredients in and blend until smooth. Take out the resulting paste and form it into cherry-sized balls in your floured hands. Put them in the fridge.

To make the soup. Sauté the diced onions and carrots in the vegetable oil in your saucepan until the onions are soft but not coloured. Add all the other vegetables, pour on the beef stock, bring to the boil and simmer for 20 minutes. Remove the oil from the surface. Drop in the dumplings and simmer for 5 more minutes. Dice the corned beef (solidified fat removed) and cook it in the soup for a further 2 minutes. Season and serve, dividing the dumplings equally between the warm bowls.

Eel Soup

Ingredients *(Serves 4/6)*

12	river eels, skins on, filleted and cut up	6	peppercorns
3	medium onions, chopped	1 tbsp	chopped capers
150g	flour		Vegetable oil
150g	butter		Juice of half a lemon
3 tbsp	allspice		Chopped parsley and tarragon
			Salt and black pepper

Method

Sauté the onions gently on your frying pan in half the butter until they begin to colour. Dust the eel fillets with some of the flour and sauté them in your saucepan in the vegetable oil until they brown slightly. Shake in 2 tablespoons each of the parsley and tarragon along with the allspice, peppercorns, capers and lemon juice. Drop in the sautéed onions, pour on 1 litre of water, bring to the boil. Skim and simmer, covered, for 30 minutes. Meanwhile, make a roux with the rest of the butter and flour in the onion pan. Remove the eels with a slotted spoon and put aside. Stir the roux into the soup, bring it back up to heat and, when it thickens, put the eels back in. Season to your taste and serve on warm soup plates, garnished with chopped parsley.

England

Chilled Cucumber Soup

Kholodniy Sup Iz Ogurtsov

In hot weather the Estonians like to eat this soup with a flaked cod salad and horseradish sauce.

Ingredients *(Serves 6/7)*

7	cucumbers, de-seeded and cut in chunks	250ml	sour cream
1	small onion, finely chopped	3	egg yolks
		65ml	dry sherry
2 tbsp	unsalted butter	30g	dill, chopped
750ml	chicken stock	Grated zest of a lemon	
		Salt and pepper	

Method

Sauté the chopped onion in the butter in a small saucepan until it is soft but not coloured. Transfer it all to your large saucepan with the cucumber and 20g of the chopped dill and cook, covered, over a medium flame for 5 more minutes, stirring from time to time. Turn up the flame and pour on the stock – gradually at first and, as it comes to the boil, add it faster. When all the stock is in, skim, turn it down to simmer, season to your taste and cook, covered, for 5 more minutes. Blend the soup with your hand blender or in batches in your liquidiser, return it to the saucepan and bring it back to simmer. Blend the egg yolks, dry sherry and sour cream, stir in a cup of the hot soup and then stir it quickly back into the saucepan. Stir in the lemon zest, turn off the heat, season to your taste and chill overnight. Whisk the soup a little before serving and garnish each serving bowl with the remaining chopped dill.

Cabbage Cream Soup *Kabsas Supp Ga Rōōsk*

Ingredients *(Serves 5)*

1	small head of cabbage, trimmed and finely chopped	1	bunch of parsley stalks, chopped to 1cm in size
2	carrots, shredded in narrow ribbons	2 tbsp	cornflour
		2 tbsp	milk
1	medium courgette, diced	150g	soft butter
400ml	double cream		Chopped dill for garnish
			Salt

Method

Simmer the cabbage and carrots in 250ml of water in your large saucepan for 20 minutes. Pour on the cream and bring it back to simmer. Drop in the diced courgette and parsley stalks, cook for 10 minutes more and season to your taste. Blend the cornflour and milk, and stir it into the simmering soup, which will thicken immediately. Serve with a heaped teaspoon of butter stirred into each bowl and garnish with chopped dill.

Helsinki
Tallinn
ESTONIA
Riga

Estonia

Bread Soup *Estonskiy Khlebniy Sup*

Ingredients *(Serves 4)*

6	slices black sourdough bread,* crusts off	50ml	cranberry juice
100g	raisins, soaked in 50ml plum brandy until plump	50ml	lime juice
		1/2 tsp	cinnamon powder
125g	pitted dried prunes	3	cloves
100g	cranberries	Whipped cream	
1	medium cooking apple, peeled, cored and sliced	Grated zest of a lemon	
		Sugar	

Method

Pour 1.25 litres of water and 125g sugar into your large saucepan and bring it to the boil. Drop in the bread and simmer until it begins to dissolve. Take out the bread with a slotted spoon and give it a quick zap in your food processor or blender, allowing it to retain some texture. Stir the bread back into the saucepan, pour in the soaked raisins and brandy, the prunes, cranberry juice, lime juice, lemon zest, cloves and cinnamon powder, and bring to the boil. Cover and simmer for 25 minutes. Allow to cool, take out the cloves and adjust the sugar content to your taste. Chill overnight and serve with a dollop of whipped cream.

* *Good pumpernickel is a reasonable substitute if you cannot find black sourdough bread.*

Beef Soup *Raavas Keitto*

Reindeer soup is usually on offer to tourists in Finland. Hunters and campers use it, too. There isn't much of this meat to be found outside the far north of Europe, but if you can find smoked reindeer, you can make a fine soup, substituting it for the beef in this recipe.

FINLAND

Helsinki

Stockholm

Tallinn

Ingredients *(Serves 8)*

1.5kg 1	eg beef, trimmed and chopped	4	waxy potatoes, cooked, peeled and cubed
1	large onion, diced	2 tbsp	plain flour +
4	carrots, chopped	2 tbsp	butter, for a roux
2	celery stalks, chopped		Vegetable oil
			Salt and black pepper

Method

Put the meat, onion and some vegetable oil in your large saucepan and brown the meat all over. Pour on 1.5 litres of water, bring to the boil, skim and simmer for 60 minutes. Drop in the carrots and celery and simmer for a further 90 minutes. Remove the saucepan from the flame, skim the fat off the soup and take out the meat. Make the roux and stir it into the soup. When the soup has thickened, stir in the meat and potatoes. Bring the soup back to heat, season to your taste and serve in large soup plates.

Fish Soup *Kalastanjan Kalakeitto*

Ingredients *(Serves 5)*

500g	fillets of any white fish or salmon	5	slices black rye bread, crusts off
3	medium onions, diced	1 tbsp	butter
1 litre	fish stock	250ml	cream
2	large waxy potatoes, cooked, peeled and cut in small cubes	3	bay leaves
		1	good pinch of allspice
			Chopped parsley

Fish Soup

Method

In a small, covered, saucepan sauté the onions in the butter, agitating from time to time until they become soft but not browned. In your large saucepan, bring the stock to the boil, drop in the fish, onion, potatoes, bay leaves and allspice and simmer for 10 minutes. Season to your taste. Remove the bay leaves and fish with a slotted spoon. Flake the fish and return it to the soup. Ladle into heated bowls over a slice of the rye bread in each and add a dollop of cream sprinkled with parsley on top.

Summer Soup

Kesä Keitto

Ingredients *(Serves 6)*

6	small new potatoes
6	baby onions, peeled
12	baby carrots
20	French beans
1.25	litres vegetable stock
50g	frozen petit pois
1	heaped tsp cornflour
Salt and white pepper	

Method

Pour the stock into your large saucepan, bring it to the boil, drop in the potatoes and onions and simmer for 15 minutes. Add the rest of the vegetables and simmer for 10 more minutes. Skim. Remove from the flame

Finland

and take out the vegetables with a slotted spoon. Cut the potatoes in two, the beans into 2cm pieces and the carrots into 1cm pieces. Put the saucepan back on the flame. Mix the cornflour with a little water and stir it into the saucepan. When the soup thickens slightly, season it to your taste, drop the vegetables back in and simmer for 3 minutes more. This soup can be served hot, but more often it is served chilled.

Pea Soup *Herne Keitto*

Ingredients *(Serves 8)*

500g	dried peas	2 litres water
1	onion, sliced	Thyme
500g	salt shoulder pork	French or English mustard
1 large	carrot, chopped	

Method
Cover the dried peas with boiling water and soak overnight. Boil the pork with the carrot, thyme and onion in your large saucepan for 60 minutes. Take the saucepan off the flame, skim off any excess fat, add the peas and simmer for another 35 minutes. Stir with a wooden spoon from time to time to prevent the peas sticking to the bottom of the pan. Allow to cool, take out the pork and cut the meat into cubes. Dispose of the fat, bone and carrot. Return the meat to the saucepan, bring it back to heat, stirring from time to time. Serve this hearty soup in warm bowls with a heaped teaspoon of the mustard of your choice stirred in.

French Onion Soup *Soupe à l'oignon gratinée*

On one of our camping holidays we were driving south to the Rhone valley and stopped at a Routier café for lunch. When the soup was being served, mine got sloshed on to my lap. An inversion, perhaps, of the cartoon, 'Waiter, there's a fly in my soup.' My two young sons enjoyed the experience more than I did.

Ingredients *(Serves 6)*

1.5 litres	clarified consommé
6	medium onions, sliced or diced finely
1	glass of dry sherry*

125g	grated Gruyère cheese
2 tbsp	butter
Salt and black pepper	

Method

Sweat the onions with the butter and a little water in your medium saucepan until soft. Transfer the onions to a large saucepan, pour on the clarified consommé, bring to the boil and add the sherry.* Simmer, covered, until there is no 'bite' in the onion – about 20 minutes. Season to your taste, ladle into bowls and serve sprinkled with the cheese.

Note: This soup can be made quite quickly by using two cans of Campbell's consommé for stock and by sweating the diced onions in your microwave oven as described on p. 13.

*   *This is the chef's choice... the French might not approve!*

France

Petite Marmite

Ingredients *(Serves 10)*

400g	lean rump beef, chopped	75g	leek, white parts only, chopped
200g	lean rib beef, chopped	2	small onions, diced
100g	marrow bone, split	50g	celery, chopped
2	lots of chicken giblets, chopped	100g	cabbage, sliced
		2.5 litres	cold consommé
100g	small carrots, chopped	Rusks	
70g	turnip, diced	Salt and white pepper	

Method

Tie the marrow bone in muslin and put it into your large saucepan, with the beef. Pour on some of the consommé, bring to the boil and skim. Drop in all the vegetables and simmer gently, uncovered, for 3 hours, pouring on more consommé from time to time to compensate for evap-  oration. Add the chicken giblets and cook for another hour. Remove the marrow bone and skim off the excess fat from the surface of the soup. Take the marrow bone from the muslin and put it back in the pot. This soup can now be seasoned and served with rusks in, or clari-fied, with the vegetables removed, and kept as a stock base for many other soups.

Potage Bourguignon

Ingredients *(Serves 8)*

420g	can haricot beans	1.75 litres vegetable stock
3 large	onions, finely chopped	Butter
4 stalks	celery, finely chopped	Salt and black pepper
2 tbsp	vegetable oil	

Method

Sauté the onion and celery with the vegetable oil in your large saucepan over a medium heat until soft but not coloured. Pour on the stock, bring to the boil and simmer covered for 30 minutes. Stir in the beans and cook for a further 5 minutes. Remove fat from the surface, season to your taste and ladle into warm bowls. Serve with a pat of butter on top in each bowl. Croutons go well with this, too.

Pot-au-Feu

The French vary this family dish from district to district by using different meats such as salt beef, pork, veal or pork-stuffed chicken with ham. Some add sausage or preserved goose (confit d'oie). Garlic, too, and a variety of vegetables can be used, though cabbage is a must in all of them.

Ingredients *(Serves 8)*

500g	lean rump beef, cut in cubes	8	small onions, skin removed
100g	marrow bone	100g	celery, chopped
1x 1kg	chicken, with the giblets chopped	150g	cabbage, sliced
200g	carrots, chopped	2 litres	cold consommé (see note on p. 73)
100g	turnip, diced		
100g	leeks, white parts only, chopped	Salt and black pepper	

Method

In your large saucepan bring the beef, marrow bone and chicken to the boil and skim. Drop in all the other ingredients, season to your taste and simmer, covered, for 60 minutes. Remove excess fat. Take out the chicken, beef and marrow bone and keep warm. Pour the soup through a colander into another saucepan, assemble the vegetables on a platter and keep warm. Reheat the soup, skim and serve as a starter. For your main course, serve the carved chicken and beef, the chopped marrow from the bone and the vegetables, accompanied with pickles of your choice and your favourite mustard.

Chicken Potage *Purée de Volaille à la Reine*

This medieval soup was served at banquets at court to honour the Queen when she was present. I suppose some earlier queen had fancied it and it became a curious gastronomic protocol.

Ingredients *(Serves 6)*

1 x 1kg	chicken	100g	long-grained rice
1 litre	chicken stock	2	egg yolks, lightly beaten
1	leek, white parts only, chopped	2 tbsp	soft butter
1	stalk celery, chopped	White pepper and salt	

Method

Pour the stock, the celery and the leek into your saucepan. Bring to the boil, lower in the chicken, skim and simmer, covered, for 30 minutes. Add the rice, skim, season to your taste and cook for 30 minutes more. Take out the chicken, allow it to cool, remove the skin and take the meat off the bone. Cut the meat up into smallish pieces, blend it to a paste with a little hot stock and 2 tablespoons of butter in your food processor or in batches in your liquidiser. Bring the soup back to simmer, stir in the chicken paste and simmer for a minute or two longer. Turn off the flame and stir in the beaten egg. This will thicken the soup to the required consistency, which is when it is ready. Croutons or rusks should be served with the soup to absorb all that butter.

Cream of Artichoke Soup
Crème d'artichauts

Ingredients *(Serves 8)*

SOUP

800ml	Béchamel sauce
250ml	chicken stock
8 large	artichoke hearts, sliced
400ml	cream

BÉCHAMEL SAUCE

80g	flour +
80g	butter, for a roux
750ml	milk
Salt and pepper	

Method

To make the Béchamel sauce. Whisk the butter into the flour over a medium heat and gradually pour on the milk, stirring all the time until you arrive at the correct consistency. Season to your taste and put aside with cling film on the surface to stop a skin forming.

To make the soup. Put the sliced artichoke hearts into your large saucepan, pour on the chicken stock and bring to the boil. Simmer, covered, for 10 minutes and blend it thoroughly with your hand blender. Gradually pour in the Béchamel sauce, blending at the same time. Serve in warm soup plates with crisp bread rolls on the side.

Lobster Bisque *Bisque d'homard*

Ingredients *(Serves 6)*

Shells	of 3 medium lobsters, cooked	1.3 litres	fish stock (optional)
		1	celery stalk, chopped
125g	lobster meat, in a medium dice	3	tbsp butter +
		2	tbsp flour, for a roux
1	medium onion, chopped	330ml	double cream
1	medium carrot, chopped	Salt and Cayenne pepper	
2	leeks, sliced	Rouille of Nice (see p. 194)	

Method

Ideally reduce the water in which the lobsters have been cooked or use fish stock if you have bought cooked lobsters.

77

Grind the lobster shells well in your food processor* and put them into your large saucepan with 1.3 litres of the stock. Bring to the boil, cover and simmer for 30 minutes.** Strain the resulting broth into a bowl, dispose of the shells and rinse and dry the saucepan. Then sauté the vegetables in butter in the saucepan until the onion is soft but not coloured – about 5 minutes. Stir in the flour, pour on the lobster broth and simmer gently for 20 minutes. Skim. Blend the soup in batches in your food processor or liquidiser and pour it back into the saucepan. Stir in the double cream and season to your taste. Bring it to serving heat and your bisque is ready to serve, with a dollop of rouille on top.

* *The secret of getting the real lobster bisque flavour lies in roasting the shells until they become brittle and then grinding them up as small as possible – almost to a sandy consistency.*
** *Some pour in a jigger of brandy at this stage. Too rich, maybe, but an option.*

Mussel Soup *Moules à la Mariniere*

Once, on a camping holiday, we diverted to Rouen to sample this soup. We sat outdoors under a canopy with about a hundred other diners slurping the same soup, not far from where Joan of Arc was burnt to death. Awful history, incredible soup.

Ingredients *(Serves 4)*

1.5kg	wild mussels, scrubbed and de-bearded (see p. 195)	2 tbsp	chopped parsley
		2 tsp	chopped thyme
2 tbsp	chopped shallots	1	small bay leaf
65g	butter, cut in small cubes	Black pepper	
		Dry white wine	

Method

Melt the butter in your medium saucepan and sauté the chopped shallots until they soften but do not colour. Drop in the thyme, bay leaf and 1 tablespoon of chopped parsley. Dispose of any open mussels and put the remainder into the saucepan. Turn up the flame and pour on enough white wine to cover the shellfish. Allow the wine to come to the boil and, when the mussels open, turn off the flame and remove the mussels with a slotted spoon. Put them in a bowl and quickly remove the top shell from each one. Divide them equally between 4 large warm soup plates with any remaining juice in the bowl. Bring the broth up to just below boiling point and ladle it into each bowl. Serve sprinkled with the rest of the chopped parsley, accompanied by plenty of crispy, well-buttered French bread.

Leek and Potato Soup *Vichyssoise*

Ingredients *(Serves 4)*

4	large leeks, white parts only, chopped	150g	butter
		400ml	cream
3	medium potatoes, peeled and sliced	Finely chopped chives	
		Freshly ground nutmeg	
1 litre	chicken stock	Salt and black pepper	

Method

Melt the butter in your medium saucepan, stir in the chopped leeks and sauté over a medium flame until soft but not brown. Drop in the potato slices and chicken stock, cover and simmer for 20 minutes. Skim, allow to cool and blend in your food processor or blender in batches until smooth. Pour back into the saucepan and bring to the boil. Add salt, pepper and nutmeg to your taste. Remove from the flame and stir in the cream at this stage, if you want to serve it hot.

Note: *To serve it chilled, keep the soup in the fridge overnight and stir in the cream before bringing it to table. Serve in bowls, garnished with chopped chives.*

Bouillabaisse à la Parisienne

Ingredients *(Serves 8)*

1	glass dry white wine	1	tomato, peeled and de-seeded
500g	red mullet, filleted (retain head, gills removed)	1	small onion, chopped
500g	whiting, filleted (retain head, gills removed)	1	leek, white part only, chopped
500g	eel (retain head, gills removed)	2	tbsp olive oil
500g	monkfish, filleted (retain head, gills removed)	1	clove garlic, crushed
		1	good pinch of saffron
500g	Dublin Bay prawns	1	bay leaf
24	mussels	1	sprig of thyme
			Parsley, chopped
			Salt and black pepper

Method

Chop the fish into bite-sized chunks, wash and beard the mussels and put both aside. In a medium saucepan, gently sauté the onion and leeks in the olive oil until they are soft but not coloured. Spoon this into your large saucepan and layer the white fish, placing the whole prawns, the mussels and the remaining ingredients (except the chopped parsley and seasoning) on top. Use the medium saucepan to bring the wine, fish heads and stock to boiling point. Then carefully pour everything into the large saucepan. Turn up the flame and cook briskly, uncovered, for 15 minutes. To serve, assemble the white fish evenly in large soup plates, topped with the whole prawns and mussels (shells on). Ladle on the broth and serve immediately. Garnish with parsley and season.

Note: *The classical way of serving this particular recipe to each diner is to put the fish with a blob of kneaded butter in a* timbale *(a metal bowl) and the broth over garlic bread in another. There are several versions to be found in France, which has long Atlantic and Mediterranean coastlines. Maybe I'm squeamish, because I leave out the fish head.*

(See page 91 for the Kakavia Fish Soup from Greece. This is similar.)

Georgian Cold Pork Soup *Mugeug1*

Ingredients *(Serves 4)*

1 kg	pig's feet, ears and tails	4	slices white bread
1	medium onion, chopped	1	garlic clove, crushed
1	small carrot, chopped	1	bay leaf
2 tbsp	white wine vinegar	1	pinch of cinnamon
		Salt and white pepper	

Method

Put all the ingredients except the salt and pepper into your large saucepan, pour on 1.5 litres of water and bring to the boil. Skim, cover and simmer gently for 2 hours. Season to your taste and take out the pork. Strain the broth into a bowl and refrigerate overnight. Before serving, take the meat from the bones, ears and tails and cut it in a dice. Divide this evenly between 4 cold soup plates. Stir up the stock, which will have turned to jelly, and spoon it over the meat.

Georgian Chilled Soup *Sup Ohlazhdennyj*

Ingredients *(Serves 4/5)*

750ml	vegetable stock	1	garlic clove, pressed or
300ml	full cream		minced
100g	cottage cheese	1 tbsp	flour
75g	raisins	White pepper and salt	
75g	dried apricots, chopped	Chopped dill, to garnish	

Method

Put the cottage cheese, cream and flour into your liquidiser. Blend smooth and put it aside. Put all the other ingredients except the dill into your large saucepan, bring to the boil and simmer for 10 minutes. Season to your taste, stir in the cream/cheese mixture and simmer, still stirring, for a few minutes more. Allow to cool and chill overnight. Serve in cold bowls garnished with chopped dill.

Georgian Dense Soup *Kashi*

Ingredients *(Serves 4)*

600g	lean beef, minced	60g	kidney fat, minced
750g	tripe, minced	30g	butter
300g	maw,* minced	4	slices of white bread, crusts off
4	garlic cloves, crushed and salted	Ground allspice or nutmeg	

Method

If you do not have a grinder, use your food processor to mince up the tripe, maw and kidney fat. Using a wooden spoon, sauté these with the minced beef in your large saucepan until well browned. Pour over

* *Craw or stomach lining of a bullock.*

83

1 litre of water, bring to the boil, skim, add in a few pinches of your preferred spice and simmer gently, covered, for 60 minutes. Take the saucepan off the flame and skim off the fat. Butter the bread and put a slice into each hot soup plate with a salted, crushed clove of garlic on top. Ladle the hot soup into each plate and serve immediately.

Georgian Spicy Beef Soup with Plums
Sup Pranyj Govadina S Slivy

Ingredients	*(Serves 8/10)*	
SOUP		Celery salt
900g	round steak, cut in 2.5cm cubes	Chopped parsley stems
		Lemon juice
2	medium onions, finely chopped	Cayenne pepper
		Coriander leaves, chopped
2	bay leaves	Salt
2	garlic cloves, crushed or minced	**SPICE BAG**
1 tsp	dried thyme	$1/2$ tsp — dried chilli flakes
3 tbsp	vegetable oil	5 — allspice berries
420g	can of chopped tomatoes, with juice	10 — peppercorns
		15 — coriander seeds
6	large plums, peeled,* stoned and diced	$1/2$ tsp — fenugreek seeds
		★ *Some like to spoon in a little plum jam at the last stage of cooking.*

Method
Tie the spices tightly in a muslin square. Sauté the onions, garlic and beef in vegetable oil in your large saucepan, stirring well until the beef colours. Pour on 1.75 litres of water, bring to the boil and drop in the spice bag. Skim and simmer, covered, for 60 minutes. Pour in the tomatoes and juice, the parsley stems, thyme, and a pinch or two of Cayenne, cover and simmer for 30 minutes more. Allow the soup to cool and put it through a strainer. Remove the beef with a slotted spoon and put it aside. Dispose of the rest of the stuff in the strainer. Chill the broth and cool the beef overnight, removing the fat before the final preparation. Reheat the broth up to simmer and add the beef, plums and a few shakes of celery salt. Pour in a little lemon juice, testing until the taste suits you. Season, again to your taste, and serve at table from a tureen into large soup plates with chopped coriander as garnish.

Potato Soup *Kartoffelsuppe*

Ingredients *(Serves 6)*

4	large waxy potatoes, peeled, cooked and diced	50g	butter
		1.5	litres chicken stock
2	celery stalks, diced	Chopped dill	
1	medium onion, sliced	Salt and black pepper	

Method

Sweat the celery and onion in the butter in a small, covered, saucepan until the onion softens. Bring the stock to the boil in your large saucepan and stir in the sweated vegetables and the potatoes. Skim, simmer for 20 minutes and season to your taste. Cook for 10 more minutes. Blend the soup with a hand blender or in batches in your food processor. Bring it back to heat and serve in large soup bowls, with a dollop of sour cream on top, sprinkled with dill.

Buttermilk and Ham Soup
Buttermilch und Schinkensuppe

Ingredients *(Serves 8)*

Ham bones or a ham hock*		500ml	buttermilk
420g	can of haricot beans	50g	butter +
2	large waxy potatoes, peeled, cooked and diced	50g	flour, for a roux
		Ginger, nutmeg or allspice to your own taste	

Method

Cover the bones or ham hock with 2 litres of water in your large saucepan, bring to the boil, skim, cover and simmer for 2 hours. Take

---

*   *If you use a ham hock, cut away the fat at the end of cooking, dice the lean meat and stir it into the soup before serving.*

Cabbage Soup

it off the flame and remove the bones or hock. Remove any excess fat. Pour in the buttermilk, add the beans and potatoes, bring back up to simmer and season with the spice of your choice. Make the roux and stir it in. Cook for 3 minutes more, stirring while the soup thickens. Serve in warm bowls.

Cabbage Soup *Kohl-Suppe*

Ingredients *(Serves 8)*

1	Savoy cabbage, trimmed and sliced	50g	flour +
		50g	butter, for a roux
1	large onion, sliced	Chopped dill	
2 litres	chicken stock	Salt and white pepper	
175ml	sour cream		

Method

Pour the chicken stock into your large saucepan and bring to the boil. Drop in the cabbage and onion, cover and simmer for 30 minutes. Skim and allow to cool. Take out the cabbage and onion with a slotted spoon and blend them with some of the soup in your liquidiser in batches. Return them to the saucepan, season and bring back to simmer. Make the roux and stir it in. When it thickens, serve very hot in bowls garnished with chopped dill and a dollop of sour cream.

Beer Soup *Biersuppe*

The capacity of Germans for quaffing huge quantities of beer is well known to me now. I used to think we Irish had a goodly reputation for knocking back light-year volumes of Guinness. My experiences in bierkellers opened – or, perhaps, closed – my eyes. They drink the stuff from steins, endlessly; thousands of folk in these huge boozing arenas. What! No alcohol in this soup?

Ingredients	*(Serves 6)*		
		2 tbsp	sugar
750ml	milk	2 x 500ml cans of beer	
3	eggs, beaten	Salt and white pepper	

Method

Bring the beer to boiling point in your saucepan to get rid of the alcohol. While it is still hot, pour it into a double-boiler, add the eggs, milk and sugar and stir well with a fork until the egg thickens and textures the soup, which will now be at drinking temperature. Season with salt and pepper or a sprinkle of ground cinnamon on each serving bowl or mug.

Hamburg Eel Soup *Hamburg Aal-Suppe*

Ingredients	*(Serves 4/6)*		
10	river eels, skins on, filleted and cut up	2 tbsp	white wine vinegar
2	large onions, chopped	1 tbsp	white sugar
150g	flour	30g	chopped sage
150g	butter	Chopped parsley	
3 tbsp	allspice	Salt and white pepper	
		Vegetable oil	

Method

Sauté the onions gently on your frying pan in half of the butter until they begin to colour. Dust the eel fillets in some of the flour, then sauté them in your saucepan in the rest of the butter until they brown slightly. Add the sage, the allspice, white wine vinegar and sugar. Drop in the sautéed onions, pour on one litre of water and bring to the boil. Skim, cover and simmer for 30 minutes. Meanwhile make a roux with the rest of the butter and flour in the onion pan. Remove the eels with a slotted spoon and put aside. Stir the roux into the soup, bring it back to heat and, when it thickens, put the eels back in. Season to your taste and serve on warm soup plates, garnished with chopped parsley.

Lentil Soup *Fakes Soupa*

Ingredients *(Serves 4)*

250g	brown lentils	420g	can of diced tomatoes, with juice
2 tbsp	tomato paste		
1	bay leaf	25ml	olive oil
1	medium onion, chopped	1 tsp	wine vinegar
		1 tbsp	dried oregano
		Salt and black pepper	

Method

Put the lentils* into your large saucepan with the oil and onions and sauté them over a medium flame, stirring frequently, until the onions are soft but not coloured – about 10 minutes. Pour on 1 litre of water, skim and bring to the boil. Add the oregano, bay leaf, tomatoes and vinegar and simmer for 30 minutes or until the lentils are thoroughly cooked, stirring with a wooden spoon from time to time to make sure the lentils do not stick to the bottom of the saucepan. Put in the tomato paste and blend the soup with your hand blender. Serve in warm bowls with croutons. Dillute with water if it becomes too thick during cooking.

* *Always rinse lentils well as they are often dried on the ground in the sun and may have tiny stones in them.*

Chickpea Soup *Revithosoupa*

Ingredients *(Serves 4)*

1 x 440g	can of chickpeas	5	peppercorns
150ml	olive oil		Chopped parsley
2	medium onions, finely		Juice of 2 lemons
	chopped		Salt

Method

Sauté the chopped onions in the oil in your large saucepan until they soften but do not colour. Add the chickpeas, peppercorns and lemon juice, and pour on 1 litre of water. Bring to the boil, add salt to your taste, skim and simmer for 15 minutes. Remove the peppercorns. Blend the soup with your hand blender and serve in warm bowls, garnished with the parsley.

Egg, Lemon and Lamb Soup

Avgolemoni Kai Arni Soupa

Ingredients *(Serves 6)*

1.5kg	leg or shoulder of lamb	1	celery stalk, finely
3	waxy potatoes, peeled,		chopped
	cooked and diced	2	onions, finely chopped
4	carrots, diced		Salt and black pepper
60g	long-grained rice		Avgolemono sauce (see p. 192)

Method

Put all the soup ingredients except the cooked potatoes into your large saucepan and pour on 1.5 litres of water. Season to your taste, bring to the boil and skim. Cover and simmer for 60 minutes. Remove the saucepan from the flame, take out the meat and keep it warm for serving as the main course. Skim the fat from the soup, add the diced potatoes and bring back up to heat. Serve in warm bowls with the Avgolemono sauce.

Kakavia Fish Soup *Soupa Kakavia*

Ingredients *(Serves 10)*

1.5	litres fish stock	2	garlic cloves, crushed
1.5kg	various Mediterranean fish, gutted and scaled, heads on*	420g	can of tomatoes, liquidised with the juice
1kg	shellfish*	1	glass of dry white wine
500g	onions, sliced thinly	250ml	olive oil
2	carrots, diced	1 tbsp	chopped parsley
1	celery stalk, sliced thinly	1	bay leaf
2	waxy potatoes, peeled, cooked and diced	Lemon juice	
		Salt and white pepper	

Method

Sauté the onion in the olive oil in your largest casserole, until soft but not coloured. Stir in the carrots, celery and garlic, and coat with the oil. Pour on the tomato, fish stock, wine, bay leaf and some salt and pepper. Bring to the boil, skim and simmer, covered, for 30 minutes. Pour the liquid through a colander into a large bowl and put the vegetables aside. Strain the liquid back into the casserole, put in the large fish first and simmer gently for 2 minutes. Then put in the remainder of the fish according to size, allowing each type to cook for 1 minute as they are added, finally putting in the shellfish in their shells, and simmering for 3 minutes more. Adjust seasoning and carefully stir in the vegetables. You are now ready to serve the soup in deep hot soup plates, garnished with chopped parsley, lemon wedges and well buttered crispy white bread on the side.

* *Use whatever sea fish are available. If you don't happen to live on the Mediterranean, try cod, hake, whiting, gurnard, monkfish, lemon sole, mackerel, mullet, bream and conger eel, for example, gutted and scaled, with heads on and gills removed. Use mussels (scrubbed, open ones rejected), prawns and shrimps put into the soup whole, i.e. shells on. Before adding the mussels, sweat them over a little water in a smaller, covered, saucepan until they open, then drop them in whole with the liquid.*

Timing is important with this soup. All the fish must be firm-fleshed when the soup is served.

SOME MEDITERRANEAN FISH AND SHELLFISH

Red mullet, rass, John Dory, anchovy, eel, haddock, sardine, squid, bonito, swordfish, dolphin, lobster, prawn, crab, shrimp, oyster, scallops, clams.

Tomato Soup

Tomato Soup *Paradicsoleves*

Ingredients *(Serves 4)*

250g	lean back rashers of bacon, diced small	2	celery stalks, sliced thinly
1	large onion, sliced thinly	1 tbsp	white sugar
2 x 220g	cans diced tomatoes		Pepper and salt
			Sour cream
			Vegetable oil

Method

Sauté the bacon in some vegetable oil in your saucepan, add the onion and celery, and cook until the onion is soft but not coloured. Pour off the fat. Pour on the tomatoes with their juice and 300ml water, and bring to the boil. Add the sugar and simmer, covered, for 45 minutes. Season to your taste and cook for a few minutes more. Skim, allow to cool and blend well in batches in your liquidiser or food processor. Return this to the pot, bring it back to heat and serve in bowls with a dollop of sour cream.

Cherry Soup *Meggyleves*

Ingredients *(Serves 4)*

750g	Morello cherries	150g	sugar
100g	sour cream	750ml	water
125g	dry red wine		Peel of half a lemon
1	egg yolk		2cm cinnamon stick
1 tbsp	flour		

Method

Pour the water and wine into your saucepan; add the sugar, lemon peel and cinnamon stick, and bring to the boil. Simmer for 10 minutes. Remove the cinnamon stick and lemon peel and stir in the cherries. Blend together the sour cream, egg yolk and flour. Bring the soup back to the boil. Turn down the flame and stir in the blended mix of cream, egg yolk and flour to thicken the soup. Cool and serve chilled.

Note: You can also try this soup with gooseberries, raspberries, blackberries or redcurrants.

Green Bean Soup *Zöld Bab Leves*

Ingredients *(Serves 6)*

1 litre	beef stock	100g	noodles
1	onion, diced	1	clove garlic, crushed
1	carrot, diced		Chopped parsley
1	green pepper, diced		Vinegar
500g	green beans, cut in 2cm pieces		Sugar
2 tbsp	tomato, peeled, de-seeded and diced		White pepper and salt

Method

Sauté the onion in a little vegetable oil until it is soft but not coloured. Bring the stock to the boil in your large saucepan, add all the other vegetables, skim, cover and simmer for 20 minutes. Skim, add the noodles and cook for another 10 minutes. Carefully add a touch of vinegar and sugar until you get a balance of flavour which suits you. Season to your taste. Take out the vegetables with a slotted spoon and share them evenly between heated bowls. Ladle the soup over them and serve, garnished with parsley.

Freshwater Fish Soup *Édesvízi Hal Leves*

Ingredients *(Serves 4/6)*

500g	small freshwater fish, gutted, for stock	1	green pepper, sliced
1kg	carp or pike, scaled and filleted	1	green pepper, diced
		420g	can of chopped tomatoes
1	large onion, sliced	1 tbsp	paprika
			Salt and Cayenne pepper

Method

Chop up the whole small fish and put them in your saucepan with any bones, head and tail you have from the carp. Add the sliced onion, sliced green pepper and the paprika, pour on 1 litre of water and bring to the boil. Skim and simmer, covered, for 40 minutes. Meanwhile, cut the carp into finger-thick slices, salt them well and put aside on a china platter. Strain the cooked stock into your saucepan. Add Cayenne pepper to your taste, the diced green pepper and the chopped tomatoes, and bring to simmer. Dab the carp fillets with kitchen paper to remove excess salt and drop them into the soup. Cover and simmer for 12 minutes, stirring from time to time. Break up the slices of carp with a wooden spoon, season to your taste and serve the soup in hot deep bowls.

Beef Soup *Marhahús Leves*

Traditionally this winter soup is the start of the meal in which the main course is the carved beef with the potatoes and vegetables cooked in the soup. These are served at table with sour cream and horseradish sauce.

Ingredients *(Serves 6)*

1kg	chuck beef in the piece	3	medium onions, skin on, each stuck with 6 cloves
6	black peppercorns		
6	medium carrots, whole	6	yellow potatoes, peeled and cut in two
3	celery stalks, halved		
3	medium parsnips, halved	150g	egg noodles
1	handful of parsley stalks, tied together	2 tsp salt	
		Vegetable oil	

Method
Brown the beef all over in your large saucepan. Pour on cold water to cover the meat (about 2 litres), bring to the boil and skim. Add the peppercorns and salt. Skim, cover and simmer for 1 hour. Add all the vegetables, except the potatoes, and the parsley stalks, cover again and simmer slowly for another 90 minutes. Put in the potatoes and simmer for 20 minutes, then the noodles and cook for 10 minutes more. Turn off the flame and skim. Take out the beef and vegetables, and keep warm. Ladle the broth and noodles into heated bowls and serve, garnished with parsley. Serve the carved beef and vegetables on a platter as another course to complete the meal.

Lamb Soup *Kjötsupa*

Ingredients *(Serves 5)*

2kg	shoulder of lamb
1	small onion, diced
3	medium carrots, cut in a 1cm dice
250g	Swede turnip, cut in a 1cm dice
60g	pearl barley

Parsley, chopped
Thyme, chopped
Salt and black pepper

Reykjavik

ICELAND

Iceland

Method

Cut the meat off the shoulder bone, remove the fat, and chop it into bite-sized chunks. Put it into your large saucepan with the bone, pearl barley, some salt and the onion. Pour on the water and bring to the boil. Skim and simmer for 45 minutes. Drop in the carrots, turnip, pepper to your taste and simmer for another 20 minutes. Take out the bone and remove any fat there is from the surface of the soup. You can serve this soup with the meat in it in large soup plates or in bowls with the meat served separately on a platter. Garnish the soup with the chopped herbs.

Halibut Soup *Lúðusúpa*

Ingredients *(Serves 4)*

Ikg	halibut steaks	2 tbsp	lemon juice
I litre	water	I tbsp	butter +
I tbsp	white wine	I tbsp	flour, for a roux
2	bay leaves	I tbsp	sugar
16	prunes, stoned and quartered	1/2 tsp	salt

Method

Bring the water to the boil, drop in the bay leaves, salt and halibut steaks, and simmer for about 10 minutes. Lift out the fish with a little of the stock and keep it warm. Strain the soup into another saucepan and cook the prunes in it for 5 minutes. Make the roux, stir it in and cook for 4 minutes more. Add the lemon juice and sugar. Serve in soup plates with the halibut on a platter on the table. You can garnish the halibut with flat leaf parsley and sliced lemon. Boiled fish without garnish, can look unappetising. Serve lots of crispy, buttered bread too.

Simple Fish Soup *Einfaldur Fiskur Súpa*

Ingredients *(Serves 8)*

250g	white fish fillet, cut in small pieces	I	celery stalk, finely chopped
250g	filleted salmon, cut in small pieces	I	small leek, white part only, sliced thinly
200g	cold water prawns	250ml	cream
2 litres	fish stock	2 tbsp	dry sherry
I	medium red onion, cut in a julienne	4 tbsp	dry white wine
		I tbsp	wine vinegar
3 tbsp	butter and 8 butter pats	Tomato paste
		Salt and pepper

Method

Sweat all the vegetables in the butter and a little water in a small, covered, saucepan for 5 minutes. Transfer this to your large saucepan, pour on the fish stock, stir in all the other ingredients except the fish and prawns, and bring to the boil. Cover and simmer for 6 minutes. Skim and stir in the fish and prawns. When it starts to simmer again, season to your taste and serve immediately, garnished with a pat of butter in each bowl.

Bacon Broth *Anraith Bagúin*

Ingredients *(Serves 8)*

900g	shoulder or collar of bacon, soaked overnight	1	sprig of thyme
2 tbsp	pearl barley	1	sprig of parsley
2 tbsp	lentils	1	bay leaf
2	medium onions, sliced	450g	potatoes, peeled and sliced
5	medium carrots, sliced	1	small cabbage, quartered
2	medium parsnips, sliced		
1	medium Swede turnip, sliced	1	leek, chopped
			Chopped parsley

Method

Drain the soaked bacon, put it into your large saucepan and cover it with 2 litres of water. Bring to the boil, skim and add barley and lentils. Simmer for 15 minutes and put in all the remaining ingredients, except the chopped parsley. Skim and simmer, covered, for 60 minutes. Remove the bacon and keep it warm. Skim fat from the broth. Serve the broth at table from a tureen, ladled on to large soup plates and garnished with chopped parsley. Serve the bacon, sliced, with a bowl of parsley sauce and vegetables as described below.

Note: You can make this soup with two ham shanks, serving the carved shanks with parsley sauce. Simmer these for 2 hours, adding the vegetables only for the last 60 minutes.

Ireland

Onion Soup *Anraith Oinniún*

Ingredients *(Serves 6)*

6	medium onions, peeled and diced	150ml medium sherry
1.5	litres beef stock	Croutons
75g	butter	Parmesan cheese, grated
		Salt and black pepper

Method

Sweat the diced onions in your medium saucepan with the butter and a little water, covered, until soft but not coloured, agitating it from time to time. Transfer this with the buttery juices into a large saucepan and pour on the stock. Bring to the boil, skim and simmer, covered, for 30 minutes. Season to your taste, add the sherry and simmer for another minute or two. Serve with croutons on each bowl of soup and grated Parmesan on the side.

Note: This is one of my recipes referred to in 'Useful Hints and Help' on page 12 of the book.

Kidney Soup *Anraith Duán*

Ingredients *(Serves 8)*

1	beef kidney	1	bouquet garni,
2 tbsp	vegetable oil		thyme and bay leaf
2 tbsp	flour	1	spice bag of 12 black
2 litres	beef stock		peppercorns
1 tsp	sugar	1 tsp	celery salt
			White pepper

Method

Skin the kidney, cut out and discard the choke (fatty core). Cut the kidney into small pieces and sauté in the heated oil until browned all over. Pour off the excess fat and stir in the flour to coat the kidney. Cook for another 2 minutes, then transfer to your large saucepan and add the stock. Drop in the bouquet garni, spice bag, celery salt and pepper. Bring to the boil, skim and simmer, covered, for 60 minutes, stirring from time to time. Remove bouquet garni and spice bag and serve.

Note: This soup is great as it stands, but a half glass of medium sherry and a squeeze of lemon juice before you take it off the flame make it even better.

Carrot Soup *Anraith Mecan Dearg*

Ingredients *(Serves 4)*

1kg	carrots, sliced	1 tbsp	lemon juice
1	large onion, finely chopped	2	pinches of sugar
6	cloves garlic, peeled	1 tbsp	butter
5	whole cloves	1 tbsp	olive oil
1 litre	vegetable stock		Cream and chopped parsley for garnish

Method

Sauté the onion, garlic and carrots in butter and olive oil in your medium saucepan until the onion is soft but not coloured. Drop in the cloves, pour on the stock and bring to the boil. Skim and simmer, covered, for 30 minutes. Take out the cloves and blend the soup well with your hand blender or in your liquidiser. Bring the soup back to the boil, add the lemon juice and sugar, season to your taste and simmer, stirring well, for a minute or two. Serve in soup plates, garnished with a flash of cream and chopped parsley.

Celeriac Soup

Celeriac Soup *Anraith Soloriac*

Ingredients *(Serves 8)*

1kg	celeriac, trimmed and cubed	60g	unsalted butter
3	celery stalks, chopped	2.5	litres chicken stock
1	large onion, chopped	1	bay leaf
2	medium potatoes, peeled and cubed	1 tsp	dried thyme
1	parsnip, chopped	2	pinches dried coriander
		420g	can of spinach
		Salt and white pepper	

Method

Melt the butter in your large saucepan and sauté the onion and celery until the onion is soft but not coloured. Stir in the celeriac and parsnip and allow them to absorb the butter for a few minutes. Pour on the stock, drop in bay leaf and bring to the boil. Skim and simmer, covered, for 30 minutes. Put in spinach, tyme and coriander and blend well with your hand blender or in batches in your food liquidiser. Bring back up to serving heat, season to your taste and serve at table from a tureen, ladling it on to large soup plates.

Spinach and Scallion Soup

Anraith Spionáiste agus Scallion

Ingredients *(Serves 6)*

2	bunches of spinach, de-stalked and chopped	35g	flour
2	bunches of scallions, chopped	3	pinches of ground nutmeg
1 litre	of milk	1	tbsp fresh mint, chopped, for garnish
60g	butter	Salt and black pepper	

Method

Melt half the butter in your large saucepan and sauté the scallions for about 3 minutes. Add the flour, stirring with a wooden spoon, to make a roux. Pour on the milk slowly, whisking all the time until the soup begins to show bubbles. In a covered medium saucepan, sweat the spinach with a little water, tossing it until the leaves wilt. Pour off any excess water and add the spinach to the soup. Season with nutmeg, salt and pepper to your taste and allow simmer for a few minutes more. Purée the soup with your hand blender or in batches in your food processor. Bring back up to serving heat and serve in warm bowls, garnished with chopped mint.

Pheasant and Leek Soup
Anraith Paisún agus Brachán

My cousin, a lady of considerable cookery skills who lives in County Wicklow, served me this simple but amazingly good soup recently. There has always been a tradition of country house cooking in Ireland which goes back in history to the time of the English occupation, when the Irish gentry were either dispossessed or integrated, usually through marriage and religious conversion, and the influence of English cooking found its way into the great houses. This soup would be typical of fare in that tradition, using local ingredients in an evolving cuisine.

Ingredients (Serves 4)

2	pheasant carcasses and the legs for stock*	I	medium potato, peeled, cooked and mashed
2	medium leeks, white part only, cut in rings	100g	butter
			Salt and black pepper

Method
Make a stock, as for chicken stock (see p. 16), using the pheasant instead of the chicken. Sweat the leeks in the butter and a little water in your medium saucepan, covered, agitating it from time to time until the leeks becomes soft. Transfer this with the buttery juice to a large saucepan, put in the mashed potato, pour on 1 litre of the pheasant stock and bring to the boil. Skim, season to your taste and simmer, covered, for 15 minutes, stirring gently from time to time to allow the potato to thicken the soup slightly. Serve in warm bowls with brown soda bread and butter on the side.

* *It is hardly worthwhile removing the sinews from pheasant legs to make them edible after cooking. I always use them in stock.*

Mutton Broth *Brat Caoireola*

Ingredients *(Serves 6)*

3	knuckles of lamb (hogget)	2	celery sticks, finely chopped
1 tbsp	split peas	2 litres	water
2 tbsp	pearl barley	1 tsp	dried thyme
2	large onion, chopped		Chopped parsley
4	medium carrots, chopped		Salt and white pepper

Method

Rinse the knuckles and put them into your large saucepan with the barley, split peas and water. Bring to the boil, skim and simmer for 30 minutes. Add thyme, carrots, celery, onions and a good pinch of salt and simmer for 30 minutes more. Add pepper to your taste and cook for a further 10 minutes. Remove the knuckles, skim off the fat and serve in hot bowls, garnished with chopped parsley.

Cockle Soup *Anraith Ruacan*

Ingredients *(Serves 6)*

60	cockles, scrubbed and washed (open ones discarded)	3 tbsp	butter +
		2 tbsp	flour, for a roux
2	celery stalks, finely chopped	200ml	cream
		600ml	milk
2	shallots, sliced finely		Chopped parsley
			Salt and white pepper

Method

Sweat the celery and shallots in one tablespoon of butter and a little water, covered, in your small saucepan for about 5 minutes. Put the cockles into your large saucepan, cover them with lightly salted water and bring them to the boil, shaking the pan from time to time. When the cockles open, take them out with a slotted spoon, remove the meat from the shells and strain the liquid. Make the roux in the bottom of your large saucepan and gradually stir in the cockle liquid and milk.

When it thickens, add the sweated celery and shallots, the cockles and 150ml of cream. Season to your taste. Stir in the parsley, cook for 2 more minutes and serve with a flash of cream on top of each bowl.

Shellfish Bisque *Bisc Shliogacha*

Ingredients *(Serves 7/8)*

750g	bodies, claws and empty shell tails of Dublin Bay prawns, well crushed	2 x 420g	cans of diced tomatoes
		1	large carrot, chopped
		1	medium onion, finely chopped
250g	dried marrowfat peas, soaked in boiling water overnight	1	glass of cooking brandy
		500ml	cream

Method

Make a stock in your large saucepan with the crushed prawn shells, carrots and onion in 1.25 litres of water, simmering, covered, for 60 minutes. Skim and strain out all the solids and pour the stock back into the saucepan. Work the canned tomatoes and their juice through a sieve with a wooden spoon to get rid of the pips and pour them into the stock, along with the drained peas. Bring to the boil, cover and simmer for 45 minutes, stirring from time to time. Pour on the brandy and simmer for 2 minutes to get rid of the alcohol. Stir in most of the cream and season to your taste. Blend the soup in batches in your liquidiser or food processor. Pour the soup back into the saucepan, bring it to serving heat and serve on soup plates with a flash of cream on top.

Lamprey Soup with Sage
Eascanna Lamprie agus Sage

Ingredients *(Serves 4/5)*

		1 dsp	(level) chopped sage
2	lamprey eels, filleted and back filaments removed,* head off, flesh cut up	5	sage leaves
		1 tbsp	chopped capers
4	medium onions, chopped	Juice of half a lemon	
150g	flour +	Salt and black pepper	
100g	butter, for a roux	Vegetable oil	

Method

Sauté the chopped onions in a little vegetable oil on your frying pan until it begins to colour. Put the onions aside and make your roux. Dust the lamprey pieces with flour and sauté them in some oil in your saucepan until they begin to colour. Drop in the onions, sage,** lemon juice and the chopped capers, pour on 1 litre of water and bring to the boil. Simmer, covered, for 30 minutes. Remove from the flame, skim off the fat and blend the soup in batches in your liquidiser or food processor. Bring it back to heat, season to your taste and serve in bowls, each one garnished with a sage leaf.

*   *The filaments of lamprey eels are toxic.*
** *Sage is seldom used in fish soups because it overpowers other flavours, but this soup and Hamburg Eel Soup (p. 88) are two I have come across which benefit from the herb.*

Shrimp Soup *Bisc Ribi Róibéis*

Ingredients *(Serves 6)*

350g	shrimps or prawns	300ml	milk
2	inner stalks of celery, finely chopped	300ml	cream
		I	glass of white wine
100g	sliced mushrooms	Salt and pepper	
600ml	fish stock	Cayenne pepper	
2 tbsp	butter		
2 tbsp	flour		

Method

Sauté the celery in butter in your large saucepan until it softens. Stir in the flour with a wooden spoon to make a roux. Pour in the stock and milk slowly, stirring all the time. Purée the celery in the soup with your hand blender. Sweat the mushrooms with some butter and a little water in a small covered saucepan and pour the lot into your soup. Bring to the boil and simmer for 15 minutes, stirring from time to time. Pour in the wine, shrimps and cream, and simmer for 5 minutes more. Season to your taste and serve in warm bowls sprinkled with Cayenne pepper.

Woodsman's Soup

Woodsman's Soup *Minestra Tagliaboschi*

This is a truly peasant soup that I came upon in Tuscany and is all the better for being just that.

Ingredients *(Serves 8/10)*

2 tsp	olive oil	1	head Swiss chard, coarsely chopped
2 × 420g	cans of tomatoes	8/10	thin slices of white bread
2	large red onions, chopped		
2 litres	chicken stock		

Salt and black pepper

Method

Sauté the onions in olive oil in your large saucepan until they begin to change colour. Drop in the chard and let it wilt. Mash the tomatoes in their juice, work them through a sieve with a wooden spoon to get rid of the pips and pour on to the stock. Cover the saucepan, bring to the boil and simmer for 45 minutes. Put a slice of bread into each serving bowl and ladle the soup over it. Pour on olive oil at the end.

Tuscan Mushroom Soup

Zuppa di Fungo Toscana

Ingredients *(Serves 6)*

6	slices of toasted garlic bread	1 litre	chicken stock
2 × 420g	cans of tomatoes in their juice, mashed up	16	fresh mint leaves
750g	cultivated mushrooms, chopped	2	large garlic cloves, crushed
1 tbsp	(heaped) dried porcini pieces	2 tbsp	olive oil

Salt and black pepper

Method

Pour boiling water over the dried porcini and allow to stand for 20 minutes. Cover the bottom of the saucepan with olive oil and add the

Italy

crushed garlic, cultivated mushrooms and 10 chopped mint leaves. Cook over a high heat, stirring all the time, for 4 minutes. Work the tomatoes through a sieve with a wooden spoon and put them into the saucepan with the porcini pieces and their liquid. Pour on the stock, bring to the boil and continue to cook over a high heat for 10 minutes. Skim, cover and simmer for 20 minutes more. Put a slice of garlic bread into each bowl and ladle on the soup. Serve garnished with a mint leaf.

Ribollita

Ingredients	(Serves 4/6)		
500g	canned cannelloni beans, with their juice	250g	black-leaf kale, shredded
1	small onion, minced	500g	beet greens, shredded
1	small carrot, minced	12	thin slices of day-old bread
1	celery stalk, minced	1	sprig of thyme
250g	waxy potatoes, peeled and diced	Olive oil	
2 tbsp	tomato paste	Salt and pepper	

Method

Sauté the minced vegetables in your large saucepan in the olive oil until the onion is soft but not coloured. Spoon in the tomato paste, the juice from the beans, kale, beet greens and diced potatoes. Pour on 1 litre of water, bring to the boil, season to your taste, cover and simmer for 20 minutes, stirring from time to time. Stir in the beans and simmer for a minute or two more. Skim. Layer the soup in a hot tureen, using a slice of bread to a ladle of soup, until the soup is absorbed.* Allow it to cool and refrigerate overnight. Reheat in your oven the following day and serve it in deep soup plates, with virgin olive oil sprinkled on top by each diner, to taste.

* *You can serve the soup at this stage, when it is called Minestra di pan. The word Ribollita means reboiled and in Tuscany the soup is renowned for being the tastier because of it.*

Ministroni

Ingredients *(Serves 8)*

420g	can of cannelloni beans	2	cloves garlic, crushed
1 litre	chicken stock	1	fistful of shredded basil leaves
1	red onion, chopped		
1	large carrot, diced	Olive oil	
2 x 420g	cans of diced tomatoes	Salt and black pepper	
100g	dried spaghetti, broken up small	Parmesan cheese, grated	
100g	freeze dried meat-filled tortellini*		

Method

Sauté the onion and carrot in 2 dessertspoons of olive oil in your large saucepan until the onion softens but does not colour. Pour on the stock and bring to the boil. Stir in the tomatoes and the basil, cover and simmer for 30 minutes. Cook the pasta in the soup according to the time stated on the packet, adding the beans 5 minutes before turning off the heat. Skim, season to your taste and serve with freshly grated Parmesan sprinkled on top.

* You can use whatever filling you prefer. There are as many versions of ministroni in Italy as there are regions. Most Italians use plain pastas but I like this one at lunchtime.

Pasta and Chickpea Soup
Minestra dei Ceci e della Pasta

Ingredients *(Serves 5)*

440g	can of chickpeas	2	whole cloves
1.25 ltrs	water	7 tbsp	extra virgin olive oil
3 tbsp	fresh rosemary, chopped	240g	egg tagliatelle
4	garlic cloves, finely chopped	Salt	

Method

Purée half the chickpeas and the whole cloves of garlic in your blender. Bring the water to the boil in your saucepan, add the purée and the rosemary. Season and simmer, covered, gently for 15 minutes and skim. In another saucepan cook the tagliatelle in plenty of salted, boiling water until it still has a 'bite' in it. Strain off the water, add the remaining chickpeas, season to taste and simmer for a few minutes more. Fry the chopped garlic in the olive oil until it crisps to a golden colour. Pour the soup into a warmed tureen, stir in the pasta and at the table ladle it into bowls and spoon some garlicky oil on each one.

Lentil Soup *Minestra di Lenticchie*

Ingredients *(Serves 5/6)*			
2	carrots, chopped	420g	can of chopped tomatoes and juice
2	celery stalks, chopped		
1	onion, chopped	250g	green lentils
1	bunch of fresh sage	4 tbsp	extra virgin olive oil
1	bay leaf	1 litre	water
		Salt and black pepper	

Method

Heat the oil in your saucepan over a medium flame. Add the onions and stir about for a few minutes. Increase the heat and add the celery, sage and carrots until the sage wilts. Then add the tomatoes, lower the heat and cook for a few minutes more. Drop in the lentils, pour in 1.25 litres of water, skim and season to your taste. Bring it back to the boil, cover and simmer for 1 hour, stirring from time to time. If it thickens too much, add some more water as it cooks. Allow to cool and blend with your hand blender or in batches in your food processor. Reheat and serve in warm bowls.

Savoy Cabbage Soup *Zuppa di Cavolo*

Way back in the 1950s, we drove from Turin to Aosta, high in the Alps to the east of Savoie. The car was a Fiat with Irish plates. So unusual, then, was the event for the local inhabitants that the four of us became celebrities for an afternoon, followed around by small children. We stayed in the local hotel and dined off this soup as a starter.

Ingredients *(Serves 4)*

1	large Savoy cabbage, trimmed and sliced	1 litre	chicken stock
200g	stale bread, cubed	50g	butter
275g	Fontina cheese, cut in small cubes	Salt and black pepper	

Method

Boil the cabbage in salted water until tender. Pour off the water. In your large saucepan, start with a layer of cabbage at the bottom, then bread, then cheese and so on, layering until you use up the three ingredients. Press down lightly with a ladle. Pour the stock into a medium saucepan and bring to the boil. Season it to your taste and then pour it over the layered ingredients. Allow it to soak for a minute or two. Meanwhile, melt the butter in a pan until it bubbles. Ladle the soup into hot soup plates and pour the bubbling butter on each one before serving.

Green Pea Soup *Minestra de Piselli*

Ingredients *(Serves 4)*

1kg	green peas, unshelled	6 tbsp	extra virgin olive oil
1 litre	vegetable stock	4	thick slices wholemeal bread, cut in 2cm cubes
1	onion, sliced thinly		
2 tbsp	Italian flat-leaf parsley, chopped	Salt and black pepper	

Method

Shell the peas and wash the pods well. Put the peas aside and soak the pods in cold water for a few hours. Drain and put them into your large saucepan with the stock and simmer until soft – about 20 minutes. Allow to cool and purée them in a blender with some of the stock. Pour the purée back in and put aside. In another saucepan, melt the butter and gently sauté the parsley and onion until the onion is soft. Add the shelled peas, cover with water and cook for about 12 minutes until the peas are tender. Meanwhile, heat the oil well in a frying pan and  brown the bread in it. Drain the resulting croutons on kitchen paper. Add the onion, parsley and pea mixture to the soup saucepan and simmer for a minute or two. Season to your taste and serve in warm bowls with the croutons.

A Sicilian Clam Soup *Fregula con Cocciula*

Ingredients (Serves 4)			
175g	fergula*	1 litre	light chicken stock
1.25g	live arselli**	90ml	olive oil
2	cloves of garlic, crushed	Chopped parsley	
125ml	tomato juice		

Method

Soak the clams in lightly salted water for about 4 hours, which will expel any sand that may be in them. Rinse them well in running water, heat them on a heavy-bottomed pan and reject any clams that do not open – they are dead and will make you ill. Discard the empty top halves, and strain the juices into the stock. Carefully sauté the garlic*** in the oil in your saucepan until it browns slightly. Discard the garlic cloves, stir in the tomato juice and simmer gently for 10 minutes. Pour on the broth, bring it to simmer, drop in the clams and the fergula. When the fergula becomes *al dente* – meaning 'with a bite', skim, stir in the parsley and serve the soup in deep hot bowls.

*	Fergula is a Sicilian egg pasta made with saffron. Use egg tagliatelle if you cannot find it.

**	Arselli are small clams, which may not be readily available far from the Mediterranean. Clams of your own choice may be used.

***	Sautéed garlic becomes bitter if overcooked.

Julian Potage *Pultes Julianae*

Relax … loosen your toga and shout 'Hail Caesar!'

Ingredients *(Serves 4)*

50g	wholemeal flour	2 tbsp	oyster sauce
250g	lean beef, minced	1 tsp	fennel seed
1 litre	beef stock	25g	butter +
1	calf's brain, cut up	25g	flour, for a roux
75ml	dry white wine		White pepper
1	lovage stalk, about 6 cms in length, chopped		Olive oil

Method

Bring the stock to the boil in your large saucepan, drop in the mince-meat, the brain and wine and simmer, covered, for 30 minutes. Skim, allow to cool and blend in your food processor or in batches in your liquidiser with the chopped lovage and fennel seeds. Bring back to boiling point in the saucepan and skim. Stir the roux into the soup with the oyster sauce and, when it thickens, season with pepper and serve on large soup plates.

Fish Soup *Cacciucco*

Ingredients *(Serves 6)*

2 litres	fish stock	12	mussels, washed and de-bearded
300g	monkfish, cut in 2.5cm chunks	1	medium onion, diced
150g	squid, cut in 2.5cm rings	4 tbsp	tomato paste
500g	spiny lobster tail, shelled and cut in 2.5cm chunks	6 tbsp	olive oil
100g	large prawn tails, shelled	2 tbsp	parsley, roughly chopped
800g	filleted cod, skin on, cut in 4cm pieces	1	red pepper, finely chopped
12	clams, scrubbed and soaked		Anise
6	scallops, shelled		Salt and white pepper

Method

Sauté the diced onion and the red pepper in the olive oil in your large saucepan until the onion is soft but not coloured. Stir in the tomato paste, pour on the stock and bring to the boil. Drop in the monkfish, lobster and squid, cover and simmer for 8 minutes. Put in the cod and simmer for 2 minutes more, then add the clams, mussels, scallops and prawn tails. Skim and simmer, uncovered, for 8 minutes. Judge the anise to your taste, spooning in a teaspoon at a time and then season, also to your taste. Serve in deep warm plates, dividing the fish equally between each before you pour on the soup. Garnish it with the roughly chopped parsley and have lots of crispy garlic-buttered ciabatta on the side.

These marvellous European soups go back to the times when Jews were forced to live in ghettos, not allowed to become involved in the professions, nor permitted to take part in politics or commerce in the countries in which they lived. They traded among themselves to make enough money to exist, buying food modestly and cooking imaginatively. They created the Yiddish ethic both in language and in their way of life.

Cabbage Soup *Kroit Zup*

Ingredients *(Serves 6)*			
500g	upper end brisket, cut up in small pieces		Juice of 2 lemons
1	medium cabbage, shredded finely	200g	sugar
1	medium onion, chopped	420g	can of whole tomatoes, de-seeded
1	sweet apple, peeled and quartered		Salt and white pepper

Method

Put the brisket and onion into your large saucepan and pour on 1.5 litres of water. Bring to the boil and simmer, covered, for 60 minutes, skimming the top from time to time. Stir in the rest of the ingredients and season to your taste. Simmer, covered, for another 60 minutes or so. Remove any excess fat. Serve at table from a tureen on large soup plates.

Note: This interesting soup is made traditionally with kosher beef, and the wonderful thing about it is the way the recipe ingredients allow for a unique sweet and sour flavour. Brisket of corned beef will do the trick, pretty well, for non-Jewish folk.

Chard Soup *Chard Zup*

Ingredients *(Serves 4)*			
1	bunch of Swiss chard leaves, trimmed and shredded	1	medium onion, finely chopped
1	waxy potato, cooked and diced	1 tbsp	extra virgin olive oil
3	cloves of garlic, crushed	1 litre	vegetable stock
		2 eggs, beaten	
		White pepper	

Method

In your saucepan sauté the onion and garlic in the olive oil until they begin to brown slightly. Pour on the stock, bring to the boil and simmer for 7 minutes. Stir in the chard and the potato and simmer for 10 more minutes. Skim, season to your taste and blend the soup with your hand blender. Bring it back up to simmer. Stir in the beaten eggs with a Paris whisk and, when they create a texture in the soup, serve it in hot bowls.

Chicken Soup with Matzo Balls
Hindle Zup Mit Matzo

This soup is basically a chicken stock that has been cooked for a long time, with vermicelli and matzo balls. It is a delicious 'cure every illness' soup.

Ingredients *(Serves 12+)*

SOUP		MATZO BALLS	
1.5kg	chicken parts*	2	eggs, scrambled
2	large carrots, chopped in large pieces	1 tbsp	root ginger, grated
1	large onion, quartered	3 tbsp	parsley, finely chopped
1	medium parsnip, cut in three pieces	1 tsp	ground black pepper
6	whole black peppers	1	clove garlic, finely chopped
120g	vermicelli, broken	200g	matzo meal*
Flat leaf parsley		2 tbsp	soft butter
Thyme		2 tsp	salt

Method

To make the soup. Put all the soup ingredients except the vermicelli into your stockpot, pour on 3 litres of water, bring to the boil and simmer gently, uncovered, for 3 hours. Take out the chicken parts, vegetables and peppercorns and dispose of them. Skim off the fat.

To make the Matzo Balls. Blend the salt, ginger, parsley, pepper and garlic into the scrambled eggs with a fork. Carefully mix the meal and butter into this until you get a stiff dough. Slowly trickle enough

* *Matzo meal is a fine grain used in kosher food.*

water into the dough to make it workable. In your floured hands, shape the dough into 16–18 walnut-sized balls and chill them in your fridge. Drop these, with the vermicelli, into the soup and simmer for 12 minutes. Serve in deep bowls and enjoy … you will never feel better, even if you weren't ill in the first place!

* *Use bones, feet, carcasses, wings, thighs, gizzards, hearts, livers and any other inexpensive parts of a chicken you can find. I'm lucky because I have a chicken-processing plant within a few miles of where I live. Most small supermarkets will oblige you with their chicken trims.*

Sautéd Garlic and Plum Tomato Soup
Gepregelt Knobl mit Floim Pomidor Zup

Ingredients *(Serves 4)*

8	plum tomatoes, de-seeded and halved	I large	onion, diced
I	large garlic bulb, cloves peeled and chopped	8 fresh	basil leaves, cut in fine ribbons
440g	canned tomatoes, with juice	I tbsp	brown sugar
200ml	vegetable stock		Olive oil
			Natural yogurt
			Salt and black pepper

Method

Sauté the chopped garlic cloves in olive oil until light brown. Grill the halved plum tomatoes until the skin blisters. Remove the skin. In your large saucepan sauté the onion in olive oil gently until it colours. Stir in the sautéed garlic and grilled tomatoes and cook for a few minutes. Shake in the brown sugar and stir until it begins to caramelise. Pour on the stock, the canned tomatoes and the juice and bring to the boil. Skim and simmer the soup, uncovered, stirring from time to time until it reduces by half. Allow to cool and blend in batches in your liquidiser or food processor. Pour the soup back into the saucepan, bring it to heat and season to your taste. Serve garnished with a flash of yogurt and basil ribbons.

Carrot and Ginger Soup *Mer und Ingber Zup*

Ingredients *(Serves 5/6)*

1 litre	chicken stock	2 tbsp	butter
4	medium carrots, peeled and sliced	250ml	dry white wine
1	large onion, chopped	1 tbsp	lemon juice
75g	grated ginger root		Garam Masala
3	cloves of garlic, chopped		Salt and pepper

Method

Sauté the ginger, onion and garlic gently in butter in your large saucepan until the onion is soft but not coloured. Pour on the stock, wine and carrots and bring to the boil. Skim and simmer, covered, for 35 minutes. Allow to cool, blend the soup in batches in your liquidiser or food processor and then pour it back into the saucepan. Spoon in the lemon juice and season to your taste, adding a pinch or so of Garam Masala powder, also to your taste. Bring the soup to heat and serve, or chill overnight and serve cold with a dribble of cream on top.

Latvian Beet Soup *Bieŝu Zupa*

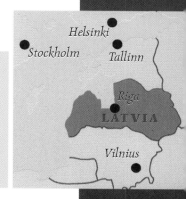

Helsinki
Stockholm   Tallinn
Riga
LATVIA
Vilnius

Ingredients *(Serves 8)*

6	large cooked beets, cut in a medium dice	4 tbsp	oatmeal
6	medium waxy pota-toes, peeled and cut in a medium dice	2 litres	beef stock
		8	hard-boiled eggs, chopped
			Sour cream
			Salt and pepper

Method

Put the diced beets, potatoes and oatmeal into your large saucepan, pour on the beef stock, bring to the boil and simmer, covered, for 20 minutes. Allow to cool, take out all the vegetables with a slotted spoon and blend them in batches in your liquidiser or food processor. Pour the soup through a sieve into a bowl and use a little of the stock to blend the oatmeal, too. Pour the stock back into the saucepan, stir in the blended vegetables and oatmeal, and bring the soup back to simmer. Put chopped egg into each hot serving bowl, ladle on the soup and serve with a dollop of sour cream.

Sour Cream Soup *Skābs Krējums Zupa*

This soup makes an interesting lunchtime dish on a hot day.

Ingredients *(Serves 4)*

250g	barley	80ml	soured milk
500ml	buttermilk	175ml	sour cream

Method

Simmer the barley in 1 litre of water in your saucepan, covered, for 60 minutes. Allow to cool to 30°C and pour in the buttermilk and soured milk (at room temperature). Pour the soup into a suitable bowl, cover it with a cloth and allow it ferment for 12 hours in a warm place. Chill overnight. Ideally, serve the soup with sour cream on top acompanied by grilled herrings and crusty bread and butter on the side.

Latvia

Potato, Beans and Mushroom Soup

Kartuplis, Pupa un Sēne Zupa

Ingredients *(Serves 6)*

240g	canned white beans
1 litre	vegetable stock
3	medium waxy potatoes, peeled and cubed
150g	mushrooms, chopped*
15	button mushrooms, finely sliced
1	medium onion, chopped

Vegetable oil
Sour cream
Chopped parsley
Salt and white pepper

Method

Sauté the chopped onion in a little vegetable oil in your large saucepan until it begins to change colour. Sweat the mushrooms, covered, in a small saucepan with some butter and, when they are ready, add them and their juices to the onion. Pour on the stock, bring to the boil, and stir in the cubed potatoes. Cover and simmer for 20 minutes. Stir in the beans and cook for 10 minutes more. Skim, season to your taste and serve sprinkled with parsley on sour cream.

* *For best results, use fresh ceps, chanterelles, morels or field mushrooms.*

Note: Try it chilled in the summer.

Latvia

Cold Beet Soup *Saltibarscial*

Ingredients *(Serves 8)*

500ml	milk, curdled with some lemon juice	1	bunch of scallions, chopped
100ml	sour cream	6	eggs, hard-boiled and diced
1	bunch of beetroot* leaves, chopped		Chopped dill for garnish
2	cucumbers, diced		

Method

Bring the milk to boiling point with a squeeze of lemon juice. When it separates, put it and the sour cream in the fridge. Pour 1 litre of water into your large saucepan, drop in the scallions and the beetroot leaves, bring to the boil, simmer for 10 minutes and allow to cool. Keep in the fridge overnight. Before serving, stir in the curdled milk, sour cream, diced cucumber and eggs. Serve in cold bowls garnished with chopped dill and accompanied by boiled new potatoes, buttered.

*   *You can also use diced cooked beetroot instead of the leaves. The Lithuanians like the taste of this soup to be quite sharp. A few squeezes of lemon juice should do the trick.*

Freshwater Crayfish Soup

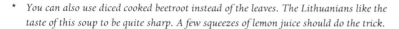

Ingredients *(Serves 5)*

500g	river crayfish tails, shelled	50g	flour, for a roux
2	cloves of garlic, chopped	50g	clarified butter*
1	medium red onion, chopped	3 tbsp	tomato purée
1	medium carrot, chopped	2 tbsp	brandy
50g	butter +	Cream	
		Salt	

Method

Simmer the crayfish tails in 1.25 litres water in your medium saucepan for 10 minutes and pour the resulting stock through a strainer into a bowl. Put the crayfish tails aside. Melt the clarified butter in the saucepan and sauté the onion until soft but not browned. Pour off the butter and add the garlic, carrot, and tomato purée. Pour on the crayfish stock and bring it to boiling point. Skim and simmer, covered, for 30 minutes. Take it off the flame, drop in the crayfish, allow to cool and purée it in batches in your food processor. Return the soup to the saucepan, bring it to the boil and stir in the roux. When it thickens, season to your taste, spoon in the brandy and simmer off the alcohol for 2 minutes. Serve in soup plates with a flash of cream on each.

*   *To clarify butter, take a Slim Jim glass and pour in hot melted butter. When the whey settles in the bottom of the glass, simply pour off the butter into a bowl, making sure to leave the whey behind.*

Pork Spareribs and Sauerkraut Soup

Gaja Riba un Sauerkraut Supa

Ingredients	(Serves 8)		
1.5	litres beef stock	250g	cabbage, finely chopped
6	pork spareribs	1	medium onion, chopped
3	pork chops	150g	Kielbasa sausage, cut in
250g	sauerkraut, rinsed and		thin slices
	squeezed dry	200g	can of chopped tomatoes
6	back rashers of smoked		Salt and black pepper
	bacon, chopped		

Method

You will need 2 saucepans for this soup. Brown the ribs and chops in your large saucepan over a medium flame, then pour the fat produced into your medium saucepan. Pour the stock over the ribs and chops and bring to the boil. Simmer, covered, for 30 minutes, take out the chops with a slotted spoon and put aside. Replace the lid and continue simmering for another 90 minutes. Remove the ribs and put aside. Season the stock to your taste and extinguish the flame. While all this is happening, sauté the cabbage, onion, bacon and sauerkraut in the fat in your medium saucepan, stirring all the time, until they soften but do not brown. Pour away the hot fat. Cut away the fat and bone from the ribs and chops and slice the meat in a small dice. For the last stage of cooking, put the large saucepan back on the flame, add the contents from the medium saucepan, the chopped meat and the canned tomatoes with the juice, and bring to the boil. Skim and simmer, covered, for 20 minutes. Then stir in the Kielbasa sausage and turn off the flame. Serve this hearty winter soup in large bowls with well-buttered crusty bread.

Macedonian Chicken Soup
Kokoshka Soupa

Ingredients *(Serves 6)*

1.5kg	chicken, jointed
125g	vermicelli
	Salt and black pepper

Chopped parsley for garnish
Avgolemono sauce (see p. 192)

Method

Put the chicken pieces, including the carcass, into your large saucepan, pour on 1.5 litres of water and bring it to the boil. Skim, season to your taste, cover and simmer for 45 minutes. Stir in the vermicelli and cook for 10 minutes more. Take the saucepan off the flame and remove the excess fat from the surface. Lift out all the chicken. Take the meat off the breast-bone and cut it in a small dice. Put this back in the soup. Discard the carcass. Cut the legs and thighs in two and keep them warm with the rest of the chicken pieces so that you can serve them with green vegetables and boiled potatoes as a main course. In Macedonia they beat egg and lemon together and blend it, drop by drop, into a bowl of hot soup, which can be tedious. Try the Greek way using Avgolemono sauce, which you spoon on to the top of each bowl of the soup as you serve it, garnished with chopped parsley.

Fruit and Nut Soup *Asure*

Ingredients *(Serves 8/10)*

250g	white beans	250g	raisins, chopped
250g	garbanzo beans	125g	filberts, crisped
250g	barley	125g	walnuts, chopped
170g	dried apricots, chopped	125g	ground almonds
90g	dried figs, chopped	200g	sugar

Method

Soak white beans and garbanzo beans in boiled water in separate bowls overnight. Boil them until soft in separate saucepans and leave

Macedonia

aside. Crisp the filberts on a heavy-bottomed pan, stirring with a wooden spoon, or roast them in your oven. Pour 2 litres of water into your large saucepan over the barley and bring to the boil. Stir in the sugar and simmer, covered, for 30 minutes. Drop in all the fruit, cover and simmer for 30 minutes more. Skim and sweeten further with sugar to your own taste. Stir in the filberts, walnuts and both varieties of beans. Allow the soup to cool and chill it overnight in your fridge. Serve in cold bowls sprinkled with on topon top ground almonds.

Chilled Curd Soup

This is an ideal soup for microwave cooking.

Ingredients (Serves 4)

1 litre	of milk	2 tbsp	tomato paste
3 tbsp	dried curd (see p. 193)	2 tbsp	natural yogurt
1	small red pepper, cut in a small dice	1	tomato, peeled, de-seeded and chopped
1	shallot, in a small dice	1 tsp	dried mint
3	cloves of garlic, cut in a small dice	Salt	

Method

Put the pepper, shallot and garlic into an ovenproof bowl with a table-spoon of water. Give it 5 minutes, covered, in your microwave at 750 power. Take it out and put it aside. Pour the milk into your medium saucepan, bring it up to boiling point and take it off the flame immediately. Stir in the curd and the tomato paste. Allow it to drop to room temperature, stir in the micro-waved vegetables, the yogurt and the tomato, and season to your taste. Keep in the fridge for at least 2 hours. Serve in cold bowls, sprinkled with dried mint.

ISLAND SOUPS

When you think about the populated islands in the seas around continental Europe, some of them now independent nations, the remainder subject to the governments of, usually, adjacent mainland countries, you find that all have one thing in common ... they are historically dominated by the cuisine in those states. Take Cyprus, for example: two states, two cuisines, Turkish in one and Greek in the other.

For this reason, I offer one island to represent the lot, namely Malta, even though Italian cuisine is dominant there. However, when it comes to what I am writing about, there are two types of soup that have been used on this almost treeless land away back into the mists of (a turbulent) history. No matter which conquering power ruled the place, the two readily available natural ingredients were rabbits and a plentiful supply of fish. Thus I offer these two truly Maltese soups, as well as the Maltese version of Minestrone to show the Italian influence.

Rabbit Soup *Fenek Soppa*

Ingredients *(Serves 6)*

2	young rabbits, boned, meat diced	2 x 420g	cans chopped tomatoes
3	large carrots, medium dice	3	cloves of garlic, crushed
3	large onions, chopped	Olive oil	
200g	lentils, soaked overnight	Salt	
		Black pepper	

Method

Make a stock with the rabbit bones in 2 litres of water in your large saucepan, simmer, covered, for 2 hours. Pour off the stock through a strainer and dispose of the bones. Heat some olive oil in the saucepan, brown the rabbit meat and remove with a slotted spoon. Drop in the vegetables and cook, stirring from time to time, until the onion softens but does not brown. Stir in the lentils, the garlic, the tomatoes and the rabbit meat, and pour on the stock. Bring it to the boil, skim and simmer, covered, for 45 minutes, stirring from time to time. Skim again, season to your taste and serve in warm bowls with slices of hopz, a Maltese bread, spread with butter or virgin olive oil.

Fish Soup *Aljotta*

Ingredients *(Serves 10)*

500g	white fish*, skinned, filleted and cut in chunks	400g	can of chopped tomatoes thinly
1 litre	fish stock	150g	cooked rice
1	large onion, chopped	1	pinch of powdered mint
1 tbsp	olive oil	Black pepper	
3	cloves of garlic, sliced	Salt	

Method

Sauté the onion in olive oil in your medium saucepan until it softens but does not colour. Pour on the fish stock and simmer, covered, for 10 minutes. Add the tomatoes and garlic, cover and simmer for a further 10 minutes. Skim off the olive oil, stir in the rice and season to your taste. Serve in warm soup plates, mint sprinkled on top, with well-buttered hopz.

* *Traditionally, going far back into the history of Malta and the nearby island of Gozo, great shoals of dolphin would appear every five or six years, to be netted by the native inhabitants, salted, dried in the sun and kept as a welcome addition to the often sparse food the land produced. Even today, 'lampuka' – the Maltese word for dolphin – is nearly always on the menu, still netted in the 21st century by the fishermen and stored in freezers. For Aljotta, any firm-fleshed white fish will do, but more often than not, lampuka is used for this soup on the island.*

Thick Vegetable Soup *Minestra*

This Maltese version of Minestrone shows the Italian influence and, of course, ground Parmesan cheese goes very well with it, shaken on top.

Ingredients *(Serves 6)*

100g	cauliflower, cut into florets and then each cut in four from the top	25g	tomato paste
		65g	long-grained rice, cooked
		1 tbsp	vegetable oil
100g	carrots in a medium dice	1.5 litres	water
1	celery stalk, chopped	Salt and black pepper	
100g	pumpkin, chopped		
100g	onion, chopped		

Method

In the bottom of your large saucepan, sauté the onion in the vegetable oil until soft but not coloured. Pour off the oil. Drop in all the vegetables and the tomato paste and pour on water. Bring to the boil, skim and simmer for 25 minutes. Season to your taste, stir in the rice, and simmer for another 5 minutes. To make sure that each diner gets his or her due, pile each soup plate high with the vegetables, using a slotted spoon, ladle on the soup and serve with well-buttered hopz.

Dutch Pea Soup *De Soep vatt de Erwt*

If ever a country has a national soup, this is the one for the Dutch. Also called Snert, it is traditionally made the day before, reheated carefully and served very thick. Sliced bacon on pumpernickel bread is generally served with it. It won't leave you hungry.

Ingredients *(Serves 6)*

1	pig's foot	2	celery stalks, sliced thinly
1	smoked ham hock	750g	split peas, soaked in hot
250g	smoked sausage,* sliced thinly		water for two hours
2	potatoes, peeled and diced	1 tsp	thyme
		1 tsp	freshly ground nutmeg
1	large onion, sliced	1 tbsp	lemon juice
		Black pepper	

Method

Parboil the pig's foot in your large saucepan for 5 minutes and pour off the water. Put in the smoked ham hock, pour on 1.5 litres of water, bring it to the boil and skim. Simmer, partially covered, for 2 hours. Meanwhile, sweat the onion and celery in a little water in a small covered saucepan for about 5 minutes, agitating it from time to time. After 2 hours, take out the hock and pig's foot, cut away the fat and discard it. Cut up the meat and put it back in the saucepan. Skim well, season the broth to your taste, and stir in everything else except the smoked sausage. Simmer for 30 minutes, stirring from time to time. Skim again, add the smoked sausage and serve on large soup plates.

*   *Cooked Kielbasa sausage is usually used in Holland.*

Dutch Beef Soup *De Soep Van Het Rundvlees*

Ingredients *(Serves 6)*

2kg	leg beef on the bone with deep meat cuts	12	button mushrooms cut in two, stalks on
2	large onions, sliced	3	medium carrots, cut in 2cm slices
420g	can of tomatoes, de-seeded, with juice	1tsp	dried thyme
180g	barley		Vegetable oil
12	small broccoli florets		Salt and black pepper

Method

Put the leg beef into your large casserole, pour on 50ml of vegetable oil and brown it all over on a medium flame. Remove the meat and pour away most of the oil and fat. Return the casserole to the flame and sauté the sliced onion until it softens but does not colour. Put in the leg beef, drop in the tomatoes, the barley and 1.5 litres of water and bring to the boil. Skim and simmer, covered, for 60 minutes. Take out the beef bones and allow them to cool. Cut away the meat, slice it into bite-sized pieces and return to the casserole. Put in the carrots and thyme, cover and simmer for 40 minutes. Skim well, stir in the broccoli florets and mushrooms, and season to your taste. Cook for 10 minutes more and serve immediately on large soup plates.

Mussel Soup *De Soep Van Mosselen*

Ingredients *(Serves 6)*

1kg	mussels, bearded (see p. 195), scrubbed and open ones discarded*	2	leeks, with 3cm green part left on, thinly sliced in rings
1	large carrot, grated	100g	butter
1	celery root, diced	250ml	fish stock
1	medium onion, thinly sliced in rings		Parsley, chopped

Method

Put the mussels into your large saucepan, pour on 1.25 litres of boiling water and bring back to the boil. Skim and simmer, uncovered, until the shells open. Take out the mussels with a slotted spoon, cut the shellfish meat from the shells and put aside. Strain the stock into a bowl and put aside. Rinse the saucepan, return it to a medium flame and sauté all the vegetables in the butter for 15 minutes, stirring from time to time with a wooden spoon. Pour on the mussel stock and the fish stock, bring to simmer, stir in the cooked mussels and season to your taste. Serve in large soup plates garnished with chopped parsley.

* *If you give a sharp tap to an open mussel shell and it closes, this shows that it is alive. If it doesn't close, throw it away immediately.*

Watergruwel

Watergruwel

Many Dutch people use this as a breakfast soup. It stores well in your fridge for a week.

Ingredients *(Serves 4)*

250g	barley	250g	raisins, soaked
250g	white caster sugar	250g	fresh cherries, pitted or
600g	fresh raspberries		glace cherries

Method

Soak the barley in 1 litre of warm water overnight and do not drain. Simmer this in your large saucepan, covered, for 1 hour. Add the sugar, raspberries and raisins and simmer for 30 minutes. Skim, stir in the cherries and simmer for 15 minutes more, stirring from time to time until you have a reasonably thick soup. Allow to cool and chill overnight.

Dutch Lentil Soup *De Soep Van De Linze*

Ingredients *(Serves 8)*

SOUP

500g lentils, well rinsed

100g bacon cubed

1 bouquet garni of mace, bay leaf and chilli pepper, tied in muslin

1 small leek, cut in rings

2 large onions, cut in rings

3 large carrots, diced

3 waxy potatoes, peeled and diced

1 bunch of parsley stalks, chopped

Vegetable oil

Salt and black pepper

MEATBALLS

250g lean beef, minced

2 slices wholemeal bread, soaked in milk

1/2 tsp freshly ground nutmeg

Fine breadcrumbs

Salt and pepper

Method

To make the meat balls. Squeeze the soaked bread free of milk and mix well with the minced beef, along with salt, pepper and nutmeg. Form

135

this into cherry-sized balls, roll them in the fine breadcrumbs and fry them in vegetable oil on your frying pan until they brown well. Drain them on kitchen paper and put them aside.

To make the soup. Sauté the bacon and all the vegetables in a little vegetable oil in your large saucepan over a medium flame for ten minutes, stirring from time to time. Spoon in the lentils. Pour on 1.5 litres water, bring to the boil, drop in the bouquet garni, skim and simmer, covered, for 30 minutes. Take the saucepan from the flame and allow to cool. Skim again and remove the bouquet garni. Blend the vegetables, bacon and lentils in batches with some of the stock in your food processor or liquidiser. Return this to the saucepan, season to your taste and bring it to serving temperature, stirring all the time. To serve, distribute the meatballs evenly between the warm soup plates, ladle the soup over them and garnish each one with chopped parsley.

Norwegian Pea Soup *Norsk Ertsuppe*

Ingredients *(Serves 6)*

500g	split peas, soaked in boiling water for 2 hours	500g	pork sausage meat
2	large onions, finely diced	1	medium potato, finely diced
1	egg, beaten		Chopped parsley
3	large carrots, finely diced		Salt and black pepper
2	celery stalks, finely diced		

Method

To make the sausage balls. Blend the egg and sausage meat together well in a bowl. Flour your hands and shape the mix into cherry-sized balls. Refrigerate.

To make the soup. Put all the vegetables and the split peas into your large saucepan, pour on 1 litre of water and bring to the boil. Skim and simmer over a gentle heat for 30 minutes, stirring from time to time. Drop in the sausage balls and simmer, still stirring as before, for 10 minutes more. If the soup becomes too thick, dilute it with water to your preferred consistency. Season to your taste before serving in warm soup plates. Garnish with the chopped parsley.

Cauliflower Soup *Blomkål Suppe*

Ingredients *(Serves 6)*

1	medium cauliflower, cut in florets	2 tbsp	butter
1	large onion, diced	250ml	milk
1 litre	chicken stock		Freshly grated nutmeg
			Salt and white pepper

Method

Sauté the onion in the butter in your saucepan until soft but not coloured. Put in the cauliflower florets, pour on the stock, bring to the boil and simmer for 20 minutes. Skim, season to your taste and blend the soup with your hand blender or in batches in your liquidiser. Pour in the milk and bring the soup back to serving temperature. Serve in hot bowls with the freshly grated nutmeg on top.

Fish Soup with Tomatoes
Fiksuppe med Tom

Ingredients *(Serves 6)*

SOUP

1.5 litres	fish stock
200g	farfalle pasta
200g	tomato paste
125g	flour +
125g	butter, for a roux
1 tbsp	chopped parsley

DUMPLINGS

1	egg
200g	self-raising flour
2 tbsp	water for a soft dough
Salt and pepper	

Method

To make the dumplings. Beat the dumpling ingredients together and form them into cherry-sized balls in your floured hands. Chill these in the fridge for 2 hours.

To make the soup. Start by making the roux in your large saucepan and pour on 250g of the fish stock, stirring, over a medium flame. When it begins to thicken, slowly pour on the rest of the stock, stirring all the time until the soup comes to the boil. Drop in the pasta, allow it to simmer and, when it becomes *al dente,** take it out with a slotted spoon and put aside in a bowl of cold water. Stir the tomato paste *into the saucepan* and simmer for a few minutes. Drop in the dumplings and, when they rise to the surface, stir the pasta back in and serve immediately, garnished with chopped parsley.

*Many pastas are of the quick cook variety these days, so check the cooking time on the box.

Chilled Blueberry Soup
Avkjøle Blueberry Suppe

Ingredients	(Serves 6)		
I	envelope gelatine	60ml	sugar
I litre	fresh orange juice	500g	fresh blueberries
3 tbsp	fresh lemon juice	Fresh mint for garnish	

Method

Dissolve the gelatine in 60ml of cold water. Mix the orange and lemon juices, then pour them into your saucepan over a low heat. When the mixture is lukewarm, stir in the sugar and gelatine, and continue stirring until the sugar has dissolved. Allow to cool and place in a bowl in your refrigerator. When it begins to become jelly, fold in the blueberries and allow to chill. Just before you serve the soup, break up the jelly with a fork and spoon it into chilled bowls. Serve garnished with mint leaves.

Orkdal Soup *Lam Suppe*

Ingredients	(Serves 4/6)		
I kg	leg of lamb, sliced and fat trimmed*	I	medium cabbage, cut vertically in four
I50g	rice	I	small onion, chopped
500g	whole carrots, trimmed	I tsp	salt

Method

Put the lamb slices into your large saucepan, pour on 1.5 litres of cold water and bring to the boil. Skim well, cover and simmer for 40 minutes. Put in the cabbage wedges and the onion, and simmer, covered, for 10 minutes. Add the carrots and cook for a further 10 minutes. Remove the lamb slices with a slotted spoon and keep warm on a platter under foil in your oven. Stir in the rice and salt, and simmer for 20 minutes. Take out the vegetables with a slotted spoon, arrange them with the meat on the platter and keep warm. Remove any fat from the soup, pour into a warm tureen and serve it at table as a starter. Serve the platter of meat and vegetables as the main course with a bowl of boiled potatoes.

*   *I like to make a gravy for the main course using 250g of the broth with a squeeze from a tube of tomato paste, a squeeze from a tube of garlic, and a shake of Worcestershire sauce, all thickened with beurre manie (see p. 193).*

In the late 1940s, when I was working in Galway City, I stayed in digs – a rented room, full meals. I shared a table with a Polish gent who had escaped the Nazi occupation and served in the R.A.F. until the end of the war. Not having much of a flair for languages, I learnt my only Polish phrase from him, phonetically. 'Brushemic kleb,' which means, 'Pass the bread.' Maybe he had a language problem, too. Once he told me, 'Always, I never smoke in chains.' So if you are taking soup with a Polish doctor (for that is what he became) you know what to say.

Galuska Soup

Ingredients (Serves 5)

SOUP

250g	chicken breast and thigh, skinned and boned
3	medium carrots, cut in 2cm pieces
1	celery stalk, chopped
1 litre	chicken stock

Chopped parsley
Salt

DUMPLINGS

1	egg
200g	self-raising flour
1 tbsp	water

Method

To make the dumplings. Beat the dumpling ingredients together and form them into cherry-sized balls in your floured hands. Chill these in the fridge.

To make the soup. Simmer all the other ingredients in a covered saucepan for 25 minutes and remove from the flame. Take out the chicken pieces with a slotted spoon, cut into a large dice and return to the soup. Bring back to simmer, drop in the dumplings and season to your taste. Skim and cook for 5 minutes more or to the point where the dumplings rise to the surface. Serve in soup plates, sprinkled with the chopped parsley.

Poland

Mushroom and Barley Soup

Mushroom and Barley Soup

Rosnać I Jeczmień Zupa

Ingredients *(Serves 8)*

100g	dried porcini mushrooms		1	celery stalk, chopped
2 litres	beef stock		25	French beans, chopped
150 g	pearl barley		1tbsp	chopped parsley
60g	butter		Sour cream	
2	carrots, diced		Salt and black pepper	
3	medium waxy potatoes, peeled and diced			

Method

Boil 100ml water and soak the dried mushrooms for 30 minutes. Take out the mushrooms, strain the water through a fine sieve and retain it. Dispose of the stalks and cut the mushrooms caps to a medium dice. Bring 500ml water to the boil in a medium saucepan, pour in the barley and simmer it gently until it absorbs the liquid (about 15 minutes), then stir in the butter. Skim, pour the beef stock and mushroom water into your large saucepan, bring to the boil and simmer, covered, for 40 minutes. Season to your taste, drop in the potatoes, celery, diced carrots and beans, and simmer for 20 minutes more. Skim and serve in bowls, with a dollop of sour cream sprinkled with chopped parsley on each.

White Borsch *Zur Soup*

Ingredients *(Serves 6)*

500g	wholemeal flour		750ml	white borsch
1	crust of wholemeal bread		4	medium potatoes, peeled, cooked and diced
750ml	vegetable stock			
30g	dried mushrooms		Salt	
1	garlic clove, crushed			

Method

White Borsch. You will need to make the basic ingedients three days ahead. Scald 500g wholemeal flour with enough boiling water to give you a thick batter. Put this in a glass jar with a crust of wholemeal bread and pour on 750g warm water. Tie the jar with gauze and leave in a warm place for 3 days to ferment.

To make the soup. Soak the dried mushroom in boiling water for 30 minutes. Remove the mushrooms, pour the liquid through a fine sieve and retain it. Remove the stalks and cut the caps in a medium dice. Bring the vegetable stock to the boil in your large saucepan and pour in the mushroom water. Add the white borsch, mushrooms, potatoes and garlic and simmer for 10 minutes. Season to your taste and serve in warm bowls.

Polish Sausage Soup *Kiełbasa Zupa*

Ingredients	(Serves 12)		
1 kg	fresh Polish sausage, cut in slices	3	large floury potatoes, cooked, peeled and cubed
1	large onion, chopped		
1	savoy cabbage, trimmed and shredded	2	clery stalks, chopped
		2 tsp	Thyme
2	large carrots, chopped	375ml	beef stock
1 tbsp	butter	1 bay leaf	
2 tbsp	wine vinegar	Salt	

Method

Melt the butter in a large saucepan and cook the sausages, onion and celery until the onion is soft but not coloured. Pour in the beef stock and add the bay leaf, vinegar, shredded cabbage, 1.25 litres of water and salt to suit your taste. Cover and cook for 30 minutes, then add the potatoes and cook for 25 minutes more. Skim and serve in warm soup plates.

My wife and I stayed in a hotel in Albufeira in The Algarve some years ago. I was intrigued to see Stone Soup on the menu and even more so to be served a watery broth with heated stones in it. How about a thought for the cavemen in the introduction to this book?

PORTUGAL
Lisbon   *Madri*

Green Soup *Verde Sopa*

Ingredients *(Serves 8)*

I tbsp	olive oil	I	green cabbage or kale, trimmed and cut in thin ribbon strips
I	clove garlic, crushed		
I	large yellow onion, chopped		
6	floury potatoes, peeled and cubed		Salt and white pepper

Method

In your large saucepan, sauté the onion, white pepper and garlic in the oil until the onion becomes soft but not coloured. Add the potatoes and cook for another 5 minutes or so. Pour on 2 litres of water, bring to the boil and simmer for 25 minutes. Blend well with a hand blender and season to your taste. Drop in the greens, put the saucepan back on the flame and simmer for about 20 minutes or until the ribbons soften. Skim and serve in bowls with a drizzle of olive oil on top.

Clam Soup *Sopa de Mexilhão*

Ingredients *(Serves 6)*

2kg	small clams	250g	frozen peas
50g	fat bacon, diced	65ml	olive oil
I	large onion, diced	I tbsp	butter
750g	rice	Parsley	

Method

If any of the clams are open, give them a sharp tap. If they do not close, throw them away. Leave the clams overnight in salted water and wash them well in two or three changes of water to make sure that no

Portugal

grit or sand remains in them. Pour the oil into your large saucepan and sauté the bacon and onion, stirring until they begin to colour. Pour on 1.5 litres of water and bring to the boil. Add the clams, parsley, peas and rice, skim and simmer gently for 25 minutes or so – the rice should be quite soft. Take off the flame and remove the parsley sprig and any loose shells with a slotted spoon. Serve the soup at table from a tureen, ladling it on to large soup plates.

Algarve Prawn Soup
Sopa do Camarão Grande Algarve

Ingredients *(Serves 5/6)*

400g	Dublin Bay prawns in the shell	1	bunch of parsley
100g	onion, diced	1 litre	fish stock
2 x 420g	can of tomatoes	3cl	brandy
50g	butter +	150cl	cream
50g	flour, for a roux	Pripiri	(see p. 195)
		Salt	

Method
Bring the stock to the boil in your saucepan, drop in the prawns and simmer for 5 minutes. Remove the prawns with a slotted spoon and allow to cool. Remove the heads. Shell the tails and return them to the saucepan. Put the heads and shells into your blender and liquidise thoroughly. Sweat the onions with butter and a little water in a small covered saucepan until soft. Return them to the soup, along with the tomatoes and parsley. Simmer for 20 minutes. Heat the blended prawn shells and heads on a pan, flame them with the brandy, put them in the soup and

146

simmer for 5 more minutes. Skim and allow to cool. Then blend the soup well in your food processor. Work the soup through a sieve with a wooden spoon over a large bowl to get rid of the shells and tomato pips. Pour the soup back into the large saucepan, add salt to your taste and the cream, and bring it up to serving temperature. Serve in warm bowls with the pripiri shaken on to taste.

Portuguese Bean Soup *Sopa de Feijão*

Ingredients *(Serves 8)*

2 x 420g	cans of red kidney beans	6	small waxy potatoes, peeled and diced
3	medium onions, chopped	1	small can of tomato paste
2	cloves of garlic, minced	1 tsp	allspice
2	bay leaves	2 litres	of vegetable stock
		Salt and white pepper	
		Bacon fat	

Method

In your large saucepan, sauté the garlic and onions in the bacon fat until they begin to brown. Pour on the stock and bring to the boil. Skim, then put in all the other ingredients and simmer for 20 minutes. Season to your taste, remove the bay leaves and serve in large bowls.

Chicken Sour Soup

Bean Soup *Ciorba de Fasole*

Ingredients *(Serves 6/7)*

250g	can of haricot, pinto or butter beans
250g	smoked bacon bones, steeped overnight
1	bunch of Swiss chard, shredded
2	egg yolks
150ml	sour cream
1 tbsp	vinegar
	Salt and pepper
	Dill, finely chopped

Method

Pour 1.5 litres of water on to the bacon bones in your large saucepan and bring it to the boil. Cover and simmer for 30 minutes. Skim, drop in the beans and the Swiss chard and simmer, uncovered, for 10 minutes more. Blend with your hand blender or in batches in your food processor. Carefully blend the egg yolks, vinegar and sour cream in a bowl and stir into the soup at just under boiling point. Season to your taste and serve immediately, garnished with the chopped dill.

Chicken Sour Soup *Ciorba de Pui Acru*

This soup is a nice soup variation. It's rather like putting vinegar into a curry dish. It gives it a bit of a bang.

Ingredients *(Serves 6)*

1.5g	chicken
6	small onions, peeled
3	medium carrots, sliced
1	bunch of parsley stalks, tied together
1	celeriac root, shredded
2	bay leaves
1/2 tsp	allspice
2	slices of stale bread
3	egg yolks
1 tbsp	vinegar
150ml	cream
	Salt and black pepper
	Dill, finely chopped, to garnish
	Savory, finely chopped, to garnish

Method

Put the chicken into your large saucepan with the bay leaves and the allspice. Pour on 2 litres of water, bring it to the boil and skim. Drop in all the vegetables and simmer, covered, for 60 minutes. Take out the chicken and the vegetables and keep warm. Discard the parsley stalks and the bay leaves. Remove surplus fat from the soup, put in the stale bread, bring back to simmer and blend it with your hand blender. Meanwhile, carefully blend the cream, vinegar and egg yolks in a bowl and stir them into the soup just below boiling point. Season to your taste. Serve the soup as a starter, garnished with chopped dill and savory. Carve the chicken and serve it as your main course with the vegetables on a platter and plenty of crispy, buttered bread on the side.

Cabbage Soup with Bacon
Ciorba Taraneasca

Ingredients *(Serves 6/8)*

300g	streaky rashers of bacon	2	egg yolks
2	onions, sliced	125ml	sour cream
2	green peppers, de-seeded and chopped	1 tbsp	vinegar
		Salt and black pepper	
20	green cabbage leaves, trimmed and cut in ribbons	Dill, finely chopped, to garnish Savory, finely chopped, to garnish	

Method
Cut up 2 slices of the bacon and fry them in the bottom of your large saucepan to produce the fat, in which you then sauté the onions and peppers until they begin to colour. Take them out of the saucepan with a slotted spoon. Chop up the remaining uncooked rashers and mix them in a bowl with the sautéed onion and green peppers. Layer the cabbage leaves, spreading each with some of the vegetable/rasher mix and seasoning, until the layering is complete. Pour on 1.5 litres of water and bring to the boil. Cover and simmer for 40 minutes. Skim off excess fat and carefully blend the cream, egg yolks and vinegar with a ladle of the soup. Turn off the flame and immediately stir the blend into the saucepan with a wooden spoon until the soup thickens. This ideal lunchtime soup, garnished with chopped dill and savory, should be served with crispy bread, cheese and pickles.

Potato Soup *Ciorba Cartof*

Ingredients *(Serves 8)*

600g	waxy potatoes, peeled and diced	1	medium onion, diced
3	medium tomatoes, skinned and de-seeded	1	bay leaf
2	medium carrots, diced	6	black peppercorns
1	bunch of parsley stalks, tied together	1	egg
			Sour cream
			Chopped parsley
			Salt

Method

Sweat the chopped onion in a small covered saucepan with a little water for 5 minutes. Pour this into your large saucepan with 2 litres of water and bring to the boil. Stir in the potatoes, carrots, parsley stalks, peppercorns and the bay leaf. Simmer, uncovered, for 30 minutes and skim. In a bowl, whisk the egg until it foams. Pour a ladle of the soup onto the egg and whisk again until they blend. Stir this blend into the simmering soup. Take out the peppercorns and bay leaf, season to your taste and serve garnished with chopped parsley and sour cream.

Fish Soup *Fish Ciorba*

Ingredients *(Serves 4)*

500g	fillets of white fish, cut in 2cm pieces	5	medium tomatoes, peeled and de-seeded
1	red pepper, de-seeded and diced	50g	cooked rice
1	green pepper, de-seeded and diced		Celery salt
1	small onion, diced		Chopped parsley and sour cream for garnish

Method

Sweat the onion and peppers with a little water in a small covered saucepan for 10 minutes. Pour these into your large saucepan with the tomatoes, rice, a good shake of celery salt, and the fish. Pour on 1 litre of boiling water and simmer for 15 minutes. Skim and serve with a dollop of sour cream sprinkled with chopped parsley on each bowl.

Borsch

My son and I got out of the taxi at Sloane Square in London to find the Russian restaurant he said was a fun place. It was the whole caboodle. We might well have been in Tolstoy's Russia. The joint jumped: vodka flowed, pretty gipsy dancers danced, the balalaika player played. There was a samovar, but who needed tea when we had the Borsch to enjoy. By the end of the night, unlike Tolstoy's character in War and Peace, we couldn't throw ourselves out the window. That's not possible in a cellar restaurant.

Ingredients *(Serves 6)*

1	large onion, sliced	1 dsp	red wine vinegar
1	parsnip, sliced	1	bay leaf
1	large carrot, sliced	50g	lard
1	large beetroot, sliced	1 tbsp	white sugar
250g	cabbage, shredded	Salt and black pepper	
1 litre	beef stock	300ml sour cream	
2 tbsp	tomato paste		

Method

In your large saucepan, sauté the onion, carrot, parsnip and beetroot in the lard over a medium flame for about 5 minutes, stirring well to coat them all in the hot fat. Pour on the stock, add the tomato paste and vinegar, and season with salt, pepper and sugar to your taste. Simmer, covered, for 30 minutes. Allow to cool, skim and blend in batches in your liquidiser or food processor. Reheat and serve in hot bowls with a flash of sour cream on each bowl.

Note: *This soup is also very good served chilled in the summer.*

RUSSIA

Helsinki
Stockholm Tallinn
Riga
Vilnius
Warsaw
Kiev
Moscow

Russia

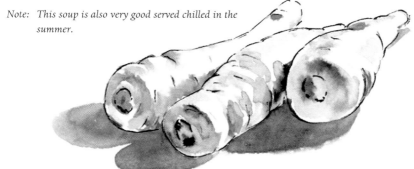

Sorrel Soup *Sup Schavel*

Ingredients *(Serves 4)*

500g	sorrel, de-stalked	2 tbsp	cream
750ml	chicken stock	1 tbsp	cornflour
1 tbsp	fennel, chopped (heaped)	2 eggs, hard-boiled and chopped	
2 tbsp	butter	Salt and Cayenne pepper	

Method

Sweat the sorrel leaves with the butter and a little water in a small covered saucepan until limp. Blend well with a little stock in your food processor. Pour this and the rest of the stock into your saucepan, season to your taste, bring to the boil, skim and simmer for 5 minutes. Mix the cornflour into the cream and stir it into the soup, which will thicken. Serve hot or cold, garnished with the chopped eggs and fennel.

Cabbage Soup *Sup Kapusta*

Ingredients *(Serves 4)*

2	onions, sliced	500ml	beef stock
2	medium beetroots, cooked and cubed	125ml	sour cream
		4	cloves
500g	cabbage, trimmed and cut into 2cm ribbons	1 tbsp	lemon juice
		1/2 tsp	dried marjoram
1	carrot, sliced	Salt	
1	parsnip, sliced		

Method

Sweat the onion with a little water in a small covered saucepan for 5 minutes. Simmer the carrot and parsnip with the cloves, onion and dried marjoram in the stock in your large saucepan, covered, for 15 minutes. Skim, put in the beetroot and simmer for 5 minutes more.

Allow to cool and remove the cloves. Blend the soup well in batches in your food processor or in the saucepan with a hand blender. Return it to the flame, add the cabbage and simmer for 20 minutes more. Skim again, season to your taste, and stir in the lemon juice. Serve in hot bowls with a dollop of sour cream on each bowl.

Barley Soup *Krupnik*

Ingredients *(Serves 6)*

250g	pearl barley		60g	mushrooms, sliced
I litre	beef stock		I	celery stalk, chopped
60g	butter, diced		I tsp	chopped dill
2	medium starchy potatoes, peeled and diced		I tsp	chopped parsley
			Salt and white pepper	

Method

Pour 250g of the stock into your large saucepan, stir in the barley, bring to the boil and allow it to simmer until the barley absorbs all the stock. Stir in the butter, piece by piece. Pour on the remaining stock, bring it back to simmer and add the potatoes, mushrooms, celery and parsley. Skim, season to your taste and simmer, covered, until the barley is tender (about 30 minutes). Beat the  sour cream until it begins to thicken and stir the dill into it. Serve the soup in soup plates with a dollop of the cream on top.

Sauerkraut Soup *Kapusniak*

Ingredients *(Serves 8)*

1kg	ham hocks	1	small tied bunch of parsley
1	medium onion, chopped	250g	sauerkraut
1	bay leaf	60g	raisins
6	peppercorns	3 tbsp	flour
2	beef stock cubes, crumbled	3 tbsp	lard
		Salt and white pepper	

Method

Put the onion, bay leaf, peppercorns and parsley into your large saucepan with the ham hocks, cover them with water and bring to the boil. Skim and simmer, covered, for 2 hours. Take out the ham hocks and allow to cool. Skim the fat off the broth and then pour the broth through a sieve. Drop in the stock cubes, and season the mixture to your taste. Remove the skin and fat from the ham hocks, carve the meat from the bones and dice it. Make a roux with the flour and lard. Return the broth to your saucepan, bring it back to the boil, add the raisins and the drained sauerkraut, and simmer for 10 minutes. Stir in the roux until the soup thickens. To serve, divide the diced ham between the hot bowls and pour over the soup.

Fish Broth *Bul'on Ryby*

Ingredients *(Serves 4)*

1kg	white fish, filleted	2 tbsp	butter
1	large onion, quartered	6	peppercorns
1	small head of Savoy cabbage, trimmed	1	bay leaf
2	carrots, chopped	Ground nutmeg	
60g	parsley stems, chopped	Salt	

Method

Brown the onion in the butter in your frying pan. Pour 1.5 litres of water into your large saucepan and bring it to the boil. Drop in the onions, carrots, chopped parsley stems, cabbage, bay leaf, peppercorns and salt to your taste, then simmer, covered, for 20 minutes. Put in the fish and simmer, uncovered, for 10 minutes more. Take out the fish and flake it. Remove the vegetables with a slotted spoon and keep them warm. Strain the broth through muslin into a bowl, return it to the saucepan and bring it back to the boil. Skim and let it reduce for 15 minutes. Add the lemon juice and nutmeg to your taste, and strain it once again. Reheat and serve it in bowls accompanied by the warmed fish and vegetables in bowls as a side dish, with melted butter and lemons cut for squeezing.

Chilled Fish Soup *Botvinya*

Ingredients *(Serves 8)*

1 kilo	white fish, filleted	Juice of half a lemon
250ml	Kvas (see p. 194)	Salt and white pepper
350g	spinach leaves	Cucumber strips, chopped
250g	sorrel leaves	scallions and grated
Sugar		horseradish for garnish
Lemon zest		Sour cream

Method

Pour 1.5 ml of water into your large saucepan over the filleted fish and bring to the boil. Simmer, covered, for 10 minutes. Take out the fish carefully with a slotted spoon and allow to cool. Cover it and put it in your fridge. Stir the spinach and sorrel into the saucepan and simmer for 5 minutes more. Take out the leaves and purée them in batches with a little of the stock in your blender or food processor. Pour the purée back into the stock, season with salt, pepper and a little sugar to your taste. Heat the mixture, sprinkle on a teaspoon of lemon zest, pour on 250ml Kvas and allow to cool. Chill in your fridge overnight. Before serving the soup, assemble the fish on a platter and garnish it with cucumber, scallions and grated horseradish. From a tureen at table, ladle the soup onto soup plates, pass around a sauceboat of sour cream and let the diners help themselves to the fish and freshly baked bread rolls, with plenty of butter.

Cock-a-Leekie

Ingredients *(Serves 8)*

1	small chicken, jointed, breasts off, all seasoned	2 tbsp	cooked rice
6	leeks, trimmed and finely chopped	2 litres	chicken stock
100g	butter		Bouquet garni
			Chopped parsley
			Salt and white pepper

Method

Put the chicken joints and breasts into your large saucepan with 75g butter, bring them up to medium heat and brown all over. Pour on the stock, put in the chicken carcass, the bouquet garni and simmer, covered, for 30 minutes. Meanwhile sweat the leeks in a covered medium saucepan with the rest of the butter and a little water for 8 minutes, agitating it from time to time. Strain the stock into a large bowl. Throw away the carcass and the bouquet garni, remove the skin from the meat and dispose of it. Take the meat off the bones and cut it in a medium dice. Skim the fat off the broth and pour it back into the saucepan. Bring it to the boil, add the diced chicken, rice and the leeks with their juice and simmer for 2 minutes. Adjust the seasoning to your taste and serve in large warm soup plates, garnished with chopped parsley.

Scotch Broth

Ingredients *(Serves 6/8)*

5	knuckles of lamb	1	small white cabbage, sliced
1	large carrot, diced		Chopped parsley
1	medium turnip, diced		Salt and white pepper
1	medium onion, diced		
3	leeks, trimmed and sliced		

Method

In your large saucepan, cover the rinsed knuckles with the water, bring to the boil, cover and simmer for an hour or so. Cut the leeks in two, lengthwise, including 2 cm of green at the top, and slice across into small pieces. Skim the broth and drop in all the vegetables. Bring it back to the boil, skim and simmer, covered, for 40 minutes. Remove the knuckles with your slotted spoon. Allow to cool and cut away the meaty bits at the joint of each. Chop these and return them to the broth. Skim well and serve very hot on large soup plates, with a garnish of chopped parsley on top of each one.

Crab Soup

This is an exceptionally good soup, well worth trying. It should impress your dinner guests no end. Some serve this soup chilled in the summer. Remember that milk burns easily when heated on the hob and will also overflow the saucepan if you let it. So go carefully.

Ingredients *(Serves 6)*

750ml	milk	750ml	chicken stock
250g	rice, uncooked	250ml	double cream
250g	crabmeat, cooked	Salt and white pepper	
3	anchovy fillets		

Method

In your heavy-bottomed saucepan bring the milk almost to the boil. Put in the rice and anchovy fillets and simmer gently for 20 minutes. Add the crabmeat and allow to cool. Blend the soup in your food processor, using a little stock to thin it. Return the soup to your large saucepan, stir in the remaining stock a little at a time and bring it to the boil. Simmer for a few minutes, stirring well. Season to your taste and serve in large soup plates with a dollop of unwhipped cream stirred in. If the soup seems too thick, thin it with milk.

Smoked Haddock Chowder

Smoked Haddock Chowder *Cullen Skink*

Ingredients *(Serves 6)*

500g	real (not dyed) smoked haddock, cut in chunks	50g	butter +
		1 tbsp	flour for a roux
500ml	milk	1 tbsp	lemon juice
500ml	water	1	bay leaf
1	medium onion, finely chopped	Chopped parsley	
		Salt and white pepper	

Method

Put the bay leaf and the haddock into your large saucepan, pour in the milk and water, and add pepper to your taste. Bring it to the boil carefully and simmer for 15 minutes. Meanwhile, sweat the onion in the butter and a little water for 10 minutes in a small covered saucepan, then stir in the flour to make a roux. Use a slotted spoon to remove the bay leaf and half the haddock chunks from the broth. Dispose of the bay leaf, flake the haddock and put it aside. Pour about 3 ladles of broth into your liquidiser with the remaining haddock and onion/flour roux and blend well until you have a paste. Bring the broth back up to simmer, skim, stir in the paste, add the lemon juice and salt to your taste, and cook for 5 minutes more. Divide the haddock flakes between 6 warmed bowls, ladle on the broth, sprinkle with parsley and serve.

Fife Broth

Ingredients *(Serves 6/8)*

125g	barley	1.5 litres water	
1kg	pork ribs	parsley	
1kg	waxy potatoes, peeled, cooked and diced	3 sage leaves	
1	onion, diced	Salt and black pepper	

Method

Rinse the barley and put it into a large saucepan with the ribs, onion, salt and sage. Pour on 1.75g water, bring to the boil, skim, cover and simmer for 2 hours. Add the potatoes and simmer for 10 minutes more.

Take out the ribs and keep them warm. Skim off all the fat, take out the sage leaves and season to your taste. Serve in hot bowls, garnished with chopped parsley, along with the ribs, presented on a platter in the centre of the table, and lots of white soda bread and butter.

Kilmany Kale

Ingredients *(Serves 6)*

1	rabbit, quartered	1	head of kale, trimmed
1	piece of salt pork	White pepper	

Method

Blanche the rabbit by covering it with water in your large saucepan, bringing it up to boiling point and then pouring off the water. Return the rabbit to the saucepan, put the pork on top with the kale, and shake on a teaspoon of pepper. Cover the ingredients with water, bring to the boil and simmer, covered, for 2 hours. Take out the rabbit, pork and kale and keep them warm. Skim the broth and serve in hot bowls, with oatcakes and butter on the side and a platter of rabbit, pork and kale in the centre of the table.

Serbian Meatball Soup

Meatball Soup *Meatball Sus Kyofte*

During the Depression in the U.S. and earlier hungry times, there was a popular song that went, 'One meat ball, one meat ball, you get no bread with one meat ball.' Meat balls are easy to make and can turn a snack soup into a meal.

Ingredients *(Serves 6)*

1.5 ltrs	chicken stock	1	egg, beaten
500g	beef or lamb, minced		Salt and pepper
1	medium onion, finely chopped		Chopped parsley
60g	cooked rice		Avgolemono sauce (see p. 192)

Method

Pour the stock into your large saucepan. Blend all the other ingredients except the Avgolemono sauce, season to your taste. Shape them into chestnut-sized meatballs in your floured hands and chill in your fridge for an hour or so. Bring the stock to the boil, drop in the cooked rice and the meatballs, season to your taste, skim and and simmer for 10 minutes. Serve with the Avgolemono sauce, each bowl, sprinkled with chopped parsley.

Serbian Bean Soup *Srpski Pasulj Supa*

Ingredients *(Serves 8-10)*

SOUP

125g	canned white beans	250ml	natural yogurt
2	carrots, peeled and diced	1 tbsp	white vinegar
2 litres	beef stock		Salt
1	parsnip, peeled and diced		
1	medium onion, chopped		DUMPLINGS
1 tbsp	lard	1	egg
2 tbsp	flour	200g	self-raising flour
3	cloves of garlic, crushed	1 tbsp	water
1 tbsp	hot paprika		

Serbia & Montenegro

Method

To make the dumplings. Blend all the dumpling ingredients in your liquidiser, shape them into cherry-sized balls in your floured hands and put them in your fridge. for 2 hours.

To make the soup. Put the carrots into your large saucepan, pour on all the beef stock and bring to the boil. Simmer for 30 minutes and stir in the beans. Melt the lard in your frying pan and sauté the onion and parsnips gently until soft. Stir in the flour with a wooden spoon and cook over a low heat until it turns to a light brown. Take the pan off the flame and stir in the crushed garlic, paprika and vinegar, and a little water to make a paste. Stir this into the soup, skim and season with salt to your taste. Add the dumplings and simmer, uncovered, for 10 minutes more, when the dumplings will have risen to the surface. Serve piping hot with yogurt spooned on top.

Sesame Chicken Soup *Sesame Pile Supa*

Ingredients	(Serves 5)		
1	small chicken, skinned, boned out and cut in bite-sized pieces	1	glass of dry white wine
		2 tbsp	sesame oil
		2 tsp	sugar
6 slices	ginger root	Salt	
1 litre	chicken stock		

Method

Heat the sesame oil in your medium saucepan until it begins to sizzle. Add the ginger and the chicken pieces, stirring them around with a wooden spoon for a minute or two. Pour off the oil, then add the wine and chicken stock. Bring to the boil and skim. Simmer gently for 20 minutes, season to your taste and add the sugar. To serve, distribute the chicken between the warm soup bowls and pour on the soup.

Christmas Soup *Kapustnica*

Like the Tuscan Ribollita, this soup improves by being cooked a few days ahead of the festival.

Ingredients *(Serves 10)*

1.5 litres	beef stock	6	cloves garlic, sliced
1.5 litres	vegetable stock	100g	dried mushroom
10	stoned prunes, halved	1	good pinch caraway seed
400g	sauerkraut	1 tsp	(heaped) dried marjoram
12	meaty pork ribs	2 tbsp	butter +
500g	pork fillet	2 tbsp	flour +
200g	smoked sausage	1 tsp	hot paprika, for a roux*
1 large	onion, diced	Salt	

Method

Before you start, soak the dried mushrooms in a bowl of boiling water for a few hours. Put the ribs and pork fillet into your large saucepan, pour on the stock (retaining 100ml) and bring to the boil. Cover and simmer for 30 minutes, then remove the pork fillet and put it aside in the retained stock. Skim the stock in your large saucepan, drop in the onion and garlic, and simmer, covered, for 60 minutes. Take the saucepan off the flame and put in the prunes, marjoram, caraway seed and mushrooms, along with the liquid in which they have been resuscitated. Return to the flame and simmer for another 30 minutes. Turn off the flame, skim again and allow the soup to cool. Remove the ribs and put aside.** Make the roux, slice the pork fillet and the sausage. Bring the soup up to boiling point and drop in the sliced pork with the roux, stirring with a Paris whisk until the soup thickens. Season to your taste and simmer for 2 minutes. The sliced sausage is stirred in just before you serve the soup in large soup plates, accompanied by generously buttered sourdough or rye bread.

*   This mix is called 'zaprazka'.
** For a fine supper dish a day or two later, shake hot paprika on the cooked spareribs, brush with honey and grill them.

Garlic Soup *Cesnakova Poliéfka*

This is a very popular soup in Slovakia because of the health-giving attributes of garlic. Simple and excellent as it is, the poached egg option makes it even better.

Ingredients *(Serves 8)*

I litre	chicken stock*	Poached eggs (optional).
I litre	vegetable stock	Parsley, chopped
8	cloves garlic, peeled	Salt
Croutons		

Method

Crush the garlic with a wooden spoon in the bottom of your large saucepan. Pour on the two stocks and bring to the boil. Simmer, covered, for 15 minutes. Season to your taste and serve in warm bowls with a poached egg in each, croutons and chopped parsley on top.

* *Some make this soup using only chicken stock.*

Mushroom Soup *Hubova Poliévka*

Ingredients *(Serves 8)*

250g	field mushrooms, cleaned and chopped up small	3 tbsp	flour +
		2 tbsp	milk, to make zatrepka*
I	large potato, cooked and cut in a small dice	50cl	vegetable oil
		Sugar and vinegar	
6	black peppercorns	Salt	
6	juniper berries		

Method

Put the peppercorns and juniper berries into your large saucepan, pour on two litres of water and bring to the boil. Spoon in the diced potato and chopped mushrooms, simmer for 30 minutes, skim, then stir in the zatrepka. When the soup thickens, season to your taste and add the vinegar and sugar, using your own judgment to achieve this unique sweet-and-sour flavoured soup.

* *Zatrepka is the Slovakian version of a French roux.*

Green Gaspacho with Shrimp

Gaspacho Verde con Los Camarones

Lisbon   Madrid

SPAIN

Spain

Ingredients (Serves 4)

500g	shrimps, shelled
1	small white turnover loaf, crusts removed
2 tbsp	white wine vinegar
3	cucumbers, peeled, de-seeded and diced
1	small onion, chopped
2 tsp	sliced almonds
2	cloves of garlic, chopped
175g	seedless green grapes
135ml	olive oil
Salt	

Method

Make breadcrumbs with half of the loaf, and cut the rest into cubes. Pour 375ml of water into a bowl with the vinegar and breadcrumbs and allow to soak for 5 minutes. Blend the cucumber, almonds, 1 clove of garlic and half the grapes in your liquidiser. Add the soaked bread crumbs, 1 teaspoon of salt and 135ml olive oil, and blend to a smooth purée. Transfer this to the bowl and chill for no less than 4 hours. Meanwhile, use the remaining olive oil to make croutons with the bread cubes in your frying pan, stirring in the shrimps and the second chopped clove of garlic for the last minute or so of cooking. Season to your taste and allow to cool. Halve the remaining grapes and mix them into this. To serve, thin the chilled soup to the consistency you like with a little cold water, pour it into bowls and garnish with the shrimp/grape/crouton mixture on top of each.

169

Gaspacho

Ingredients *(Serves 4)*

250g	cucumber, peeled, de-seeded and diced	I tbsp	fresh chives
I	red onion, sliced very thinly	I tbsp	fresh basil
		I tbsp	fresh marjoram
2	tomatoes, peeled and de-seeded	I	clove garlic
		I	green pepper, de-seeded and sliced
125ml	olive oil		Juice of a lemon
750ml	stock*		125g breadcrumbs
I tbsp	fresh chervil		Salt and black pepper
I tbsp	fresh parsley		

Method

Coarsely chop all the herbs and put them into your liquidiser with the tomatoes, garlic, pepper and lemon juice. Switch on and pour in all the olive oil in a thin stream until it is absorbed and all the ingredients emulsify. Transfer this to a bowl and slowly, with care, stir in the stock. At this stage, season to your taste. Chill overnight. Serve the soup in 4 cold soup plates, stir in the diced cucumber and sprinkle the top of each with the breadcrumbs.

* *The purists insist that water should be used, but vegetable stock makes for a more satisfying result.*

Cream of Almond Soup
Crema de la Sopa de la Almendra

Ingredients *(Serves 6*

150g	ground almonds	2 tbsp	butter
2 tbsp	slivered almonds, toasted	250ml	full cream
I	crushed clove of garlic		Few pinches of dried mace
I	inner celery stalk, minced		Celery salt and black pepper
750ml	chicken stock		

Method

Sauté the celery and garlic in the butter in your saucepan until soft but not coloured. Pour in the chicken stock with the almonds and mace and bring to the boil. Simmer, covered, for 30 minutes, stirring from time to time. Skim, allow to cool and blend in batches in your liquidiser or food processor. Pour it back into the saucepan, stir in the cream, season to your taste and bring it to serving temperature – it must not boil.

Chestnut Soup *Sopa de la Castaña*

Ingredients *(Serves 5/6)*

400g	chestnuts, peeled	1.25	litres vegetable stock
1	medium onion, chopped	40ml	soured cream
1	celery stalk with leaves, chopped	30g butter	
		Croutons	
1	clove garlic, chopped	Salt and black pepper	

Method

Sauté the onion, celery and garlic in the butter in your saucepan until they become soft and are turning a golden colour. Pour on the stock, bring to the boil, skim and season to your taste. Add the chestnuts and simmer, covered, for 30 minutes. Allow to cool and liquidise in batches until smooth. Reheat in the saucepan and serve with a flash of sour cream on top of each bowl, with croutons on the side.

Galacian Black Bean Soup
Soupa de Habas Negras de Galacian

Ingredients *(Serves 6/7)*

250g	black beans, soaked overnight in boiling water	2	cloves of garlic, chopped
1.25	litres chicken stock	2 tbsp	olive oil
2	medium onions, chopped	1 tbsp	ground cumin
2	green peppers, de-seeded and chopped	Dry sherry	
		Salt and black pepper	

Method

Sauté the onions, pepper and garlic in the olive oil in your large saucepan until soft and beginning to colour. Pour on the stock, season to your taste and bring to the boil. Skim, add the beans and cumin, and simmer for 30 minutes or until the beans are soft. Blend the soup with your hand blender or in batches in your food processor. Bring it back to serving temperature, stir in sherry to your taste and serve piping hot.

Catalan Fish Soup *Sopa de Pescado Cataluna*

Ingredients *(Serves 4)*

500g	white fish fillets, cut in medium chunks*	1	medium onion, diced
1 tbsp	flaked almonds, toasted	2	garlic cloves, finely chopped
1 tbsp	pine nuts, toasted	1 tsp	saffron threads
540ml	fish stock +	1 tbsp	olive oil
1 tbsp	fish sauce		Chopped parsley
1	glass dry white wine		Salt
420g	can of chopped tomatoes, with juice		

Method

Grind the toasted almonds and pine nuts in your food processor or with a mortar and pestle. Sauté the garlic and chopped onion in your large saucepan with the olive oil until the onion softens but does not colour. Stir in the almond and pine nut mix and cook for 1 minute. Pour in the wine and cook for 1 minute. Pour on the fish stock / the fish sauce and bring to the boil. Skim, add the fish and the saffron, and simmer gently, uncovered, for 6 minutes. Take out the fish with a slotted spoon and distribute it evenly in hot deep soup plates. Season the soup to your taste, ladle it on the fish and serve immediately with a chopped parsley garnish.

* *Use firm-fleshed fish, such as cod, monkfish, halibut or turbot.*

Basque Cod Soup *Porrusalada*

I remember well a time when salt cod could be found hanging from the ceilings of many grocery shops in inland towns and villages in Ireland. They were required to fill a religious need on Fridays, which were Fast Days. Fresh fish was seldom available outside coastal towns and cities. How many died in the mid-19th century Potato Famine in a country surrounded by seas full of fish and rivers and lakes similarly rich?

Ingredients *(Serves 8/10)*

250g	salt cod, soaked over-night and cubed	1	large onion, finely chopped
375g	white leeks, finely chopped, with some green kept for garnish	2	large waxy potatoes, peeled and diced
		100ml	extra virgin olive oil
		Cream, lightly whipped	

Method

Put all the white chopped leeks and the diced onion into a medium-sized saucepan with half the olive oil and a little water and sweat them, covered, over a flame for about 10 minutes, agitating from time to time. Transfer them to your large saucepan, add the diced potatoes, and pour on 2 litres of water. Bring to the boil, skim and simmer, covered, for 30 minutes. Remove the lid, drop in the cod and the rest of the olive oil, simmer for 10 minutes more, stirring gently from time to time. Serve in hot deep bowls, with a flash of cream, garnished with the chopped green leeks on top.

173

Cadiz Fish Soup *Sopa de Pescada Cadiz*

Ingredients *(Serves 4)*

500g	firm white fish, filleted and cut in thick slices	1	large onion, finely chopped
750ml	fish stock		Juice of 2 Seville oranges*
6 tbsp	extra virgin olive oil		Coarse salt and white pepper
3	garlic cloves, peeled		

Method

Cover the fillets with coarse salt and allow to stand for 60 minutes. Then rinse and drain them, and put aside. Heat the oil in your saucepan and sauté the garlic cloves until they turn light brown. Discard the garlic, stir in the chopped onion and sauté until soft but not coloured. Pour on 375ml of the stock, bring to the boil, skim and simmer, covered, for 15 minutes. Put in the fish and the rest of the stock and simmer, uncovered, for 8 minutes more. Break up the fish slices in the soup into bite-size pieces, pour on the orange juice and allow to stand for 10 minutes before serving in hot deep bowls.

* *The juice of one small lemon and one small sweet orange will do if Seville oranges are out of season.*

Pea Soup *Svensk Ärt Soppa*

Ingredients *(Serves 6/8)*

250g	yellow split peas, soaked overnight	50g	butter
1.5	litres fish stock	2	medium onions, chopped
3	medium carrots, chopped	1 tsp	ginger powder
2	stalks of celery, chopped		Croutons
4	medium leeks, chopped		Salt and white pepper

Method

In your large saucepan, sauté the onions and leeks with the butter until soft but not coloured. Add the strained soaked split peas, carrots, celery and ginger, pour on the stock, bring to the boil and simmer, covered, for 30 minutes. Skim and allow to cool. Blend the soup with a hand blender or in batches in your liquidiser or food processor. Pour the soup back into the saucepan, season to your taste, bring it to the boil and stir for a minute or so. Serve in warm bowls with croutons.

Nettle Soup *Nässla Sop*

There is a remarkable similarity between nettles as a soup ingredient and spinach. The differences are that, although nettles sting, you don't have to pay for them. Be daring: wear gloves when you go out a-picking.

Ingredients *(Serves 6)*

25	young nettle leaves	3tbsp	butter +
3	eggs, hard-boiled	3tbsp	flour, for a roux
1.5	litres beef stock		Salt and pepper
40g	chives		

Method

Blend the nettle leaves and chives in a little stock in your liquidiser. Pour it into your saucepan with the rest of the stock, bring it to the boil and simmer for 20 minutes. Skim and stir in the roux with a Paris whisk. When the soup thickens, season to your taste and let it bubble for a few minutes. Serve in warm bowls, ladling the soup on to half of a hard-boiled egg.

Salmon Soup *Laxen Soppa*

Ingredients *(Serves 6)*

SOUP

1 litre	stock
250ml	cream
2	egg yolks
50g	cooked carrot from stockpot, diced
50g	baby peas, cooked
1 tbsp	butter +
1 tbsp	flour, for a roux
½ tsp	salt
Chopped dill or parsley for garnish	

STOCK

1 kg	salmon trimmings from your fish shop
1	large carrot, diced
1	onion, peeled and diced
1	medium leek, white part only, chopped
5	sprigs dill
5	sprigs parsley
6	black peppercorns
Allspice	

Method

To make the stock from the salmon trimmings. Remove the gills from the head (they give a bitter flavour), chop the bones and cover with 1 litre of water. Add all the other ingredients and simmer gently for 20 minutes only. Skim and remove all the solids and bones.

To make the soup. Strain the stock into your large saucepan and bring to the boil. Put in all the soup ingredients except the roux and egg yolks. Allow to simmer for 10 minutes. Stir in the roux with a Paris whisk and add any bits of salmon meat you can find on the bones. When the soup thickens, take it off the flame, skim well and stir in the egg yolks immediately. Serve the soup in warm bowls, garnished with chopped parsley or dill.

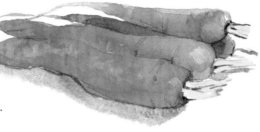

Pine Nut Soup *Tyna Bort Nöt Soppa*

Ingredients *(Serves 4)*

100g	pine nuts	3	egg yolks
250ml	chicken stock		Cayenne pepper
250ml	cream		

Method

Blend the pine nuts and egg yolks in your liquidiser to a smooth paste, pour on 125ml of the chicken stock and blend it in. Pour this mix into your double-boiler,* add in the rest of the stock and the cream, stirring all the time it is over the flame. When the soup thickens, it is ready to serve, with a shake of Cayenne pepper on top of each bowl.

* *Alternatively, you can use a saucepan held carefully above a low flame, without allowing the soup to come to the boil... it will curdle if it boils.*

Fennel Soup with Shrimps
Fennel Soppa med Räkan

Ingredients *(Serves 4/5)*

500g bulb fennel, trimmed and finely chopped	125ml soured cream
Fennel leaves, finely chopped	250ml dry white wine
100g shrimps or small prawns	2 tbsp Pernod
250ml chicken stock	Salt and black pepper

Method

Put the chopped fennel into your large saucepan, pour on the white wine and stock, and bring them to the boil. Simmer, covered, for 10 minutes. Allow to cool. Blend this in batches in your food processor or liquidiser and pour it back into the saucepan. Bring it back to simmer, drop in the shrimps and cook for 1 minute. Pour in the Pernod and simmer for 1 minute to burn off the alcohol. Stir in the sour cream and season to your taste. Serve garnished with the chopped fennel leaves.

Swiss Dumpling Soup

There wasn't much travelling abroad when I was a young fellow. There was this war going on and my part of Ireland was neutral. We could have gone to other neutrals, I thought, like Switzerland, flying in a Tiger Moth, or Sweden, Spain and Portugal, by sea. However, being shot down or torpedoed didn't appeal to my imagination. We had no exotics for sale when it came to food, but most ate well. The poor got what were called halfpenny dinners: good soup and stew for less than a cent in today's money.

Swiss Dumpling Soup *Knödelsuppe*

Ingredients *(Serves 4)*

SOUP		50g	self-raising flour
1 litre	beef stock	3 tbsp	Parmesan, grated
		3 tbsp	chopped parsley
DUMPLINGS		100ml	water
1	egg, beaten well	1/2 tsp	salt
1 tbsp	butter		

Method

To make the dumplings. Melt the butter in your small saucepan, add the water and salt, and bring to the boil. Stir in the flour and keep stirring until the dough forms a ball. Take the saucepan off the flame, mash in the egg with a fork until it combines with the dough, then do the same with the parsley and Parmesan. Make cherry-sized dumplings in your floured hands. Refrigerate for an hour or so.

To make the soup. Bring the beef stock to the boil in a larger saucepan, drop in the dumplings and, when they rise to the surface, share them equally between 4 warm bowls, ladle on the stock and serve.

Switzerland

Basel Flour Soup *Mehlsuppe Uber Basle*

Ingredients *(Serves 4)*

3 tbsp	butter	110g	butter
150g	white flour		Emmenthal cheese, grated
1	litre beef stock		Salt and white pepper

Method

Melt the butter in your frying pan over a medium flame, sift on the flour and, stirring with a wooden spoon, cook it until it turns to a golden brown. Stir in some of the stock and, when it thickens, pour it into a saucepan and stir in the rest of the stock. Bring to the boil and simmer for 20 minutes, stirring from time to time. Skim, season to your taste and serve in warm bowls with the grated cheese.

Barley Soup *Gerstesuppe*

Ingredients *(Serves 4)*

125g	ham, diced	1	small cabbage, finely shredded
125g	lean rump steak, diced		
90g	barley	3tbsp	cream +
125g	waxy potatoes, peeled and diced	1 tbsp	(heaped) flour
		1 tsp	celery salt
25g	canned haricot beans		White pepper

Method

Place the barley in your large saucepan, bringing to the boil in 1 litre of water and simmer, covered, for 30 minutes. Put in the ham, rump steak, potatoes, shredded cabbage and the celery salt, cover and simmer for 30 minutes more. Skim. Blend the flour and cream and stir it into the saucepan, along with the haricot beans and white pepper to your taste. When it thickens, serve very hot in large soup plates with crusty batons of white bread and butter on the side.

Squash Soup *Zerquetschensuppe*

Ingredients *(Serves 4)*

1	large vegetable marrow, peeled, de-seeded and diced	5g	flour
		35g	butter
1 litre	vegetable stock		Parmesan cheese, grated
60ml	milk +		Bread and butter for toast

Method

Cook the diced marrow in salted water in your saucepan until soft. Pour off the excess water and blend the marrow in batches in your liquidiser. Pour it back into the saucepan, add in the vegetable stock and bring to the boil. Blend the milk and flour with the butter and stir into the soup. Simmer for 30 minutes, stirring from time to time. Skim and serve with Parmesan cheese and buttered toast on the side.

Stuffed Lettuce Soup *Stopftegrünersalatsuppe*

Ingredients *(Serves 6)*

6	lettuce heads, whole, washed thoroughly in salt water	1.5	litres beef stock
		2	eggs, beaten
300g	lean veal, well chopped	175g	breadcrumbs
2 tbsp	cooked sweetbreads, chopped	2 tbsp	fresh marjoram, chopped
			Croutons
2 tbsp	Parmesan, grated		Salt and white pepper

Method

Lightly brown the chopped veal and sweetbreads in a little vegetable oil in your frying pan and allow to drain on kitchen paper. Put the lettuces into a large bowl and pour boiling water over them. Take them out after 40 seconds with a slotted spoon and let them drain thoroughly. Soak the breadcrumbs in a little milk until milk is absorbed, but not runny. Blend in the eggs, marjoram, Parmesan and season to your taste. Open up each soaked lettuce and put 2 tablespoons of this mixture into its centre. Carefully twist the lettuce leaves around the filling and tie them at the top with light kitchen string. Bring the beef stock to simmer in your large saucepan and lower in each stuffed lettuce with the slotted spoon. Drop in the drained chopped veal and sweetbreads, and simmer gently for 10 minutes. Skim. To serve, put a stuffed lettuce in each hot soup plate and ladle over the soup, with croutons and an extra bowl of grated Parmesan on the side.

Vegetable Soup with Cracked Wheat

Only recently I learnt that turkeys are named after Turkey. The reason for this is that Guinea fowl were first imported from Africa into Europe through that country and were known as Turkey birds. Perhaps some brainbox among the Mayflower Pilgrims who landed on Plymouth Rock saw this American bird and decided that it was the same as the Turkey bird ... hence today's model.

I suggest using the Jewish recipe for chicken soup on page 118 without the matzo balls if you want to make a post-Christmas turkey soup. Just use the carcass and whatever leftover scraps you have. If you have kept the giblets, including the neck, it will be all the better for it.

Vegetable Soup with Cracked Wheat
Bulgur Çorba

Ingredients *(Serves 10)*

2	large carrots, shredded	100g	prepared bulgur (cracked wheat)
2	medium onions, diced		
2 × 420g	cans diced tomatoes, with juice	3 tbsp	butter
		2 tsp	tomato paste
3	medium green peppers, cut in a small dice	1.5	litres chicken stock
		Salt and white pepper	

Method

Sauté the diced onions and peppers in butter for 10 minutes over a medium flame in your large saucepan, then work the bulgur in well. Pour on the stock and bring it to the boil. Stir in the shredded carrots and the tomatoes, cover and simmer for 30 minutes. Spoon in the tomato paste and cook for a few minutes more. Skim, season and serve at table from a tureen.

Anchovy Soup *Hamsi Çorba*

Ingredients *(Serves 4)*

250g	fresh anchovies, filleted	2 tbsp	flour, for a roux
I	medium onion, diced small	I litre	fish stock
		I egg	
30g	butter	2 tbsp	lemon juice
40g	carrot, cut in a small dice	I tsp	thyme
2 tbsp	butter +	Salt	

Method

Sauté the diced onion and carrot in 30g butter in your medium saucepan until the onion becomes soft but not coloured. Stir in the anchovies, pour on the fish stock and bring to the boil. Cover and simmer for 15 minutes. Allow to cool, take out the anchovies with a slotted spoon and blend them in a little of the stock in your liquidiser, along with the fresh thyme. Pour this into the saucepan and bring it back to simmer. Skim, blend the egg and lemon juice, season the soup to your taste and thicken it with the roux. Stir in the egg and lemon blend in a thin stream just before serving or in the Greek way with Avgolemono sauce see p. 192). Both are equally good.

Turkish Fish Soup *Balik Çorba*

Ingredients *(Serves 8)*

SOUP		125g	flour, for a roux
1.5kg	fillets of white fish, skin off*	Salt	
		SAUCE	
1.25	litres fish stock	250ml	lemon juice
250ml	court boullion	4	egg yolks, well blended
125ml	olive oil +		with the lemon juice

Method

Make a roux with the flour and olive oil in a medium saucepan. Pour the fish stock and the court boullion into your large saucepan and bring to the boil. Add the fish, cover and simmer for 10 minutes. Remove the fish with a slotted spoon and break it up into flakes. Stir a few ladles of the hot stock into the medium saucepan on the flame and when it begins to thicken, stir it into the large saucepan and simmer until that thickens. Stir in the flaked fish and serve on warm soup plates with the sauce stirred in.

* *Use a firm-fleshed fish. Cod or haddock are very suitable.*

Wedding Soup *Dūğūn Çorba*

Ingredients *(Serves 4)*

SOUP		Vegetable oil	
250g	lean mutton, cut in a small dice*	Salt	
		Mild paprika	
500g	mutton bones		
2 tbsp	butter +	SAUCE	
2 tbsp	flour, for a roux	2	egg yolks
I	large carrot, diced	2	tbsp lemon juice
I	large onion, diced		

Method

To make the sauce. Blend the eggs and lemon juice and put aside.

To make the soup. Sauté the meat, onion and carrot in some oil in your large saucepan until the meat browns. Put in the bones, pour on 1 litre of water and bring to the boil. Skim, cover and simmer gently for 2 hours. Remove the bones with a slotted spoon, skim off any oil from the surface and season with salt to your taste. Make the roux in another saucepan and stir in a ladle of hot soup which will become very thick. Stir this into the large saucepan and, when the broth thickens, take it off the flame and quickly stir in the egg/lemon sauce. Sauté the paprika in butter on a pan until it browns and spoon it on top of each bowl of soup just before serving.

* *Since mutton is generally unavailable nowadays, buy hogget (lamb which is one year old).*

Red Lentil and Vegetable Soup

Sepzeli Kirmizi Mercimek Çorba

Ingredients (Serves 4/6)

I litre	beef stock	I	medium carrot, grated
200g	red lentils, rinsed	I	green pepper, diced
I	medium waxy potato, peeled and grated	2 tbsp	tomato paste
I	medium tomato, skinned, de-seeded and diced		Chopped fresh mint
			Salt

Method

Pour the stock into your large saucepan, stir in the tomato paste and the mint, and bring to the boil. Add the lentils, diced green peppers, grated vegetables, cover and allow simmer for 45 minutes, stirring from time to time. Skim. If you think the lentils are absorbing too much of the stock, dilute the soup with boiling water to a consistency that suits you. Drop in the diced tomato a few minutes before you take the saucepan off the flame. Season and serve in warm bowls.

Dawn Soup *Şafak Çorba*

Ingredients (Serves 5/6)

500g	tomatoes, skinned and chopped	2 tbsp	butter, for a roux
I litre	chicken stock	4	egg yolks
2 tbsp	flour +	250ml	milk
			Salt

Method

Melt the butter with the flour in your saucepan and stir with a wooden spoon until it begins to colour. Stir in the stock, bring to the boil, season to your taste, cover and simmer for 30 minutes, stirring from time to time. Skim and strain the soup into a bowl and pour it back into the saucepan. Blend the egg yolks and milk in your liquidiser and stir this mixture into your soup, allowing the soup to come up to just below boiling point.* Take the saucepan off the flame and serve in warm mugs.

* *If you allow the soup to boil, the eggs will curdle.*

Rice Soup *Pilav Çorba*

Ingredients *(Serves 5/6*

100g	lean beef, minced	2 tbsp	tomato paste
1 litre	beef stock		Vegetable oil
1	large waxy potato, peeled and diced		Chopped parsley for garnish
150g	long-grained rice		Salt

Method

Sauté the minced beef in a little vegetable oil in your large saucepan until it browns, then stir in the tomato paste. Pour on the stock, bring to the boil, stir in the rice and simmer for 15 minutes. Drop in the diced potatoes, cover and simmer for 15 minutes more. Season with salt to your taste, skim and serve garnished with chopped parsley.

Yogurt Soup with Orzo
Yogurt Çorba Ile Orzo

Ingredients *(Serves 4)*

100g	orzo*	3 tbsp	flour
300ml	natural yogurt		Vegetable oil
1 litre	chicken stock		Chopped coriander
1	medium onion, diced		Salt

Method

Sauté the diced onion in your large saucepan until it becomes soft but not coloured. Add the coriander and stir with a wooden spoon until the onion browns. Pour on the stock, bring to the boil and simmer for 15 minutes. Cook the orzo *al dente* – meaning 'with a bite', in 500ml of water in a smaller saucepan. Meanwhile, blend the yogurt, flour and some salt to a paste and stir it into the stock immediately. Allow to simmer, uncovered, for 2 more minutes, stirring all the time. Skim, add in the drained orzo and salt to your taste, and serve in large warm soup plates.

* A Greek rice-shaped pasta. Use long-grained rice if not available.

Spinach Soup *Ispanak Çorba*

Ingredients *(Serves 4)*

80g	lean beef, minced	2 tbsp	tomato paste
200g	spinach, chopped		Vegetable oil
125g	long-grained rice		Salt and black pepper
1	small onion, diced		Natural yogurt

Method

Sauté the onion and the beef in a little vegetable oil in your medium saucepan until it browns. Stir in the tomato paste and pour on 1 litre of water. Bring to the boil and skim. Drop in the rice, cover and simmer for 20 minutes. Sweat the spinach with a little water, covered, in a smaller saucepan until it wilts. Drop this into the soup, season to your taste and simmer for 10 minutes more. Skim and blend it with your hand blender or in batches in your liquidiser. Bring it back to heat and serve in hot bowls with a flash of yogurt on top of each bowl.

Chilled Tomato Soup *Sogut Domates Çorba*

Ingredients *(Serves 6)*

3 x 240g	cans large tomatoes	250ml	natural yogurt, whipped to a creamy consistency
2 tbsp	lemon juice		Parsley, chopped
2 tbsp	olive oil		Madras curry powder
2 tbsp	white wine vinegar		Salt

Method

Liquidise the tomatoes, lemon juice, vinegar and olive oil with 1 to 2 teaspoons of curry powder in 2 batches and pour them into a bowl. Stir in the yogurt well and season to your taste. Chill for at least 2 hours. Serve in chilled bowls, garnished with chopped parsley.

Ukrainian Mushroom Soup *Sup Griby*

Ingredients *(Serves 4)*

STOCK

1	large carrot, chopped
1	medium onion, sliced
2	celery stalks, chopped
4	sprigs of parsley
1 tsp	salt

SOUP

500g	fresh field mushrooms, sliced
2 tbsp	flour
75g	butter
2 tsp	dill
2 tsp	chopped parsley
150ml	sour cream

Method

To make the stock. Pour 1 litre of water into your large saucepan and bring to the boil. Add the carrot, onion, celery, parsley and salt, cover and simmer for 30 minutes. Skim and remove all the vegetables and the parsley with a slotted spoon and dispose of them.

To make the soup. Sweat the mushrooms with the butter for 5 minutes in a smaller covered saucepan and then pour them with their liquid into the stock. Blend the flour into 40ml of water. Bring the stock up to simmer, stir in the dill and parsley, then stir in the flour/water blend. Simmer, still stirring, for 3 minutes more. Beat the sour cream until it begins to thicken and serve the soup in warm bowls with a dollop of sour cream on top.

Ukraine

Welsh Leek Soup *Cymraeg Cenhinen Botes*

Ingredients (Serves 6)

500g	leeks, white parts only, trimmed	1.5	litres chicken stock
60g	butter	250ml	cream
2	celery stalks, diced		Salt and white pepper
1	large onion, diced		

Method

Split the leeks lengthwise and slice across thinly. Soak these in cold water for 20 minutes. Melt the butter in your large saucepan and sauté the onion, leek and celery until soft, but not coloured. Pour in the stock, bring to the boil, skim and simmer, covered, for 30 minutes. Allow the soup to cool, then blend it in your liquidiser or with your hand blender. Pour it back into the saucepan, bring it up to heat and stir in the cream. Simmer for 10 minutes more and season to your taste. Serve in warm bowls.

Lobscows

Ingredients (Serves 6)

500g	lean salt beef in the piece	4	large waxy potatoes, peeled, cooked and diced
2	large onions, diced	12	slices of white bread with butter
2	medium carrots, diced		White pepper
1	medium-sized swede turnip, cubed		

Method

Put the salt beef, onions and carrots into your large saucepan, pour on 1.5 litres of water, bring to the boil, skim and simmer, covered, for 30 minutes. Add the turnip and simmer for 15 minutes more. Take out the beef and carve it. Keep the slices warm. Drop the potatoes into

the soup, stirring well, bring it to heat and simmer for a minute or two. Serve in large soup bowls sprinkled with pepper, with hot salt beef sandwiches, crusts on.

Granny's Broth *Cawl Mamgu*

In the old days, Cawl was traditionally served as dinner for the farmers during the winter months in south and west Wales.

Ingredients *(Serves 6)*

I kg	neck of lamb (hogget)*	6	medium carrots, cut in halves vertically
2	large leeks, white and green parts, chopped		Chopped parsley
I	small swede turnip, cubed		Salt and pepper
500g	small waxy potatoes		

Method

Put the neck of lamb into your large saucepan with the carrots and the white parts of the leeks, pour on 1.5 litres of water and bring to the boil. Skim and simmer, covered, for 2 hours. Allow to cool. Ladle the fat from the surface into your fat separator in batches, dispose of the fat and pour the broth back into the saucepan. Bring it back to boiling point. Drop in the potatoes, the swede turnip and simmer, covered, for 15 minutes. Add the chopped green parts of the leeks, Skim, season to your taste, and simmer for 10 more minutes. Remove the neck of lamb, put it on a serving platter surrounded with the potatoes and vegetables, and keep warm in your oven. Serve the broth in large bowls garnished with chopped parsley, and well-buttered crusty bread on the side, followed by the lamb and vegetables on the platter as the main course.

* *Lamb which is one year old.*

Some Additional Short Recipes and Cookery Terms

AVGOLEMONO SAUCE

Ingredients
  Juice of 2 lemons
  2 eggs

Method

There are two ways to make Avgolemono sauce. The first is simply to beat the eggs and lemon juice together well until the sauce foams. The second is to separate the eggs and beat the yolks into the lemon juice for the sauce. Then beat the whites in another bowl until they peak. Spoon this on top of the soup, after the sauce has been poured in.

QUENELLES

Ingredients
  250g filleted fish or meat of choice
  300ml cream, chilled
  1 egg white, whipped to soft peak

Method

Purée the fish in your food processor or liquidiser and put it in a bowl into your fridge for 2 hours. Very carefully work the whipped egg into the purée with a spatula and then the chilled cream, until they are absorbed. Use a teaspoon to shape the quenelles and drop each one into a pan of simmering water and cook for 6 minutes. Pour away the water. The quenelles will keep, covered, in the fridge for up to a week. The same method can be used for chicken or meat quenelles but these are usually presented in the form of small sausages, shaped with your floured hands, in the soup.

DRIED CURD

Method

Curd is also known as cottage cheese. Dried curd comes in various forms. In most recipes in this book, cottage cheese will do the trick if it has been pressed in a strainer with a wooden spoon to get rid of excess liquid. Cottage cheese is made by putting rennet* into milk and straining it through muslin, leaving the whey that is the cheese.

* An agent for separating milk into curd and whey in cheese making.

ROUX

Ingredients
  125g butter
  125g plain flour

Method

Melt the butter in a small saucepan and stir in the flour with a wooden spoon. Once blended, you can use it while still hot as a thickening agent. When cold, it becomes *buerre manie,* which you can keep in your fridge and use by crumbling it into soup or any other hot liquid you wish to thicken.

ROUILLE OF NICE

Ingredients
  2 tsp cayenne pepper
  3 cloves of garlic
  250ml olive oil
  2 egg yolks
  1 level tsp saffron threads

Method

Blend the garlic and egg yolks in your liquidiser, adding the cayenne pepper and saffron. Then pour in the olive oil in a thin stream at full power until it thickens to a mayonnaise consistency. Transfer it to a bowl, cover it and put it in your fridge where it will keep indefinitely

KVAS

Ingredients
  1 litre hot water
  250g beetroot, thinly sliced
  The whole crust of a rye bread loaf

Method

The kvas must be made a week in advance of using it in any soup. Pour the hot water over the sliced beetroot in your casserole. Add the crusts, cover with a cloth and let it stand in a cool corner for 7 days. Drain off the clear juice and use it as a base for the soup. Store the rest of this water in a sterilised jar in your fridge where it will be usable for 2 weeks. You can also buy kvas in food shops that specialise in Polish and Russian food.

SMETENA
This is what sour cream is known as in Poland and Russia.

SEASONING
In this book the word 'season' refers to using pepper and salt as a flavouring.

KOHLRABI

This is a vegetable of the cabbage family, with a bulbous stem, picked young and much used much in Polish cookery for its delicate nutty flavour.

POLENTA

This maize meal is much used in Italian cuisine. It is used as a thickening agent in soups but is eaten more often as a porridge with various flavourings.

PRIPIRI

This is a pepper and olive oil sauce from Portugal which you will find in top class delicatessens or supermarkets.

HOPZ

The national bread of Malta.

DE-BEARDING

This is what is done to mussels in cooking preparation. The beard is the fibrous growth with which it attaches itself to the place it lives. This must be cut away.

MUSHROOMS

For best flavour in soups, morel, cep, chanterelle and field mushrooms are recommended. Forced flats, not in the same league, may be used for flavour and forced button mushrooms, thinly sliced *look* good in soup. Dried porcini mushrooms are highly recommended too where the recipe calls for dried mushrooms.

GLAZED ONIONS

This is done when pearl onions are boiled and then glazed with butter on the pan.

Index